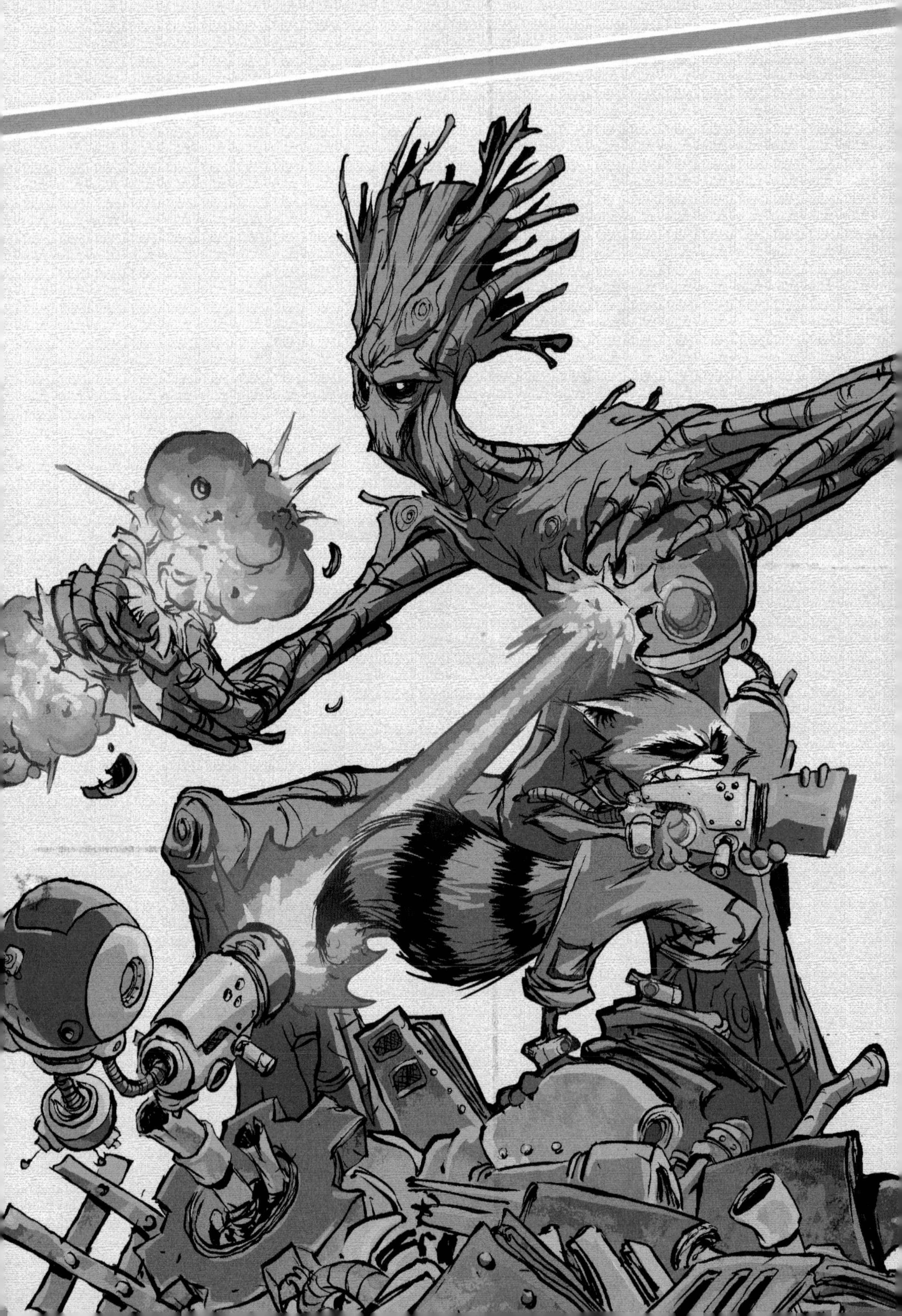

ROCKET RACCOON

A CHASING TALE

WRITER
SKOTTIE YOUNG

ARTISTS
SKOTTIE YOUNG (#1-5)
& JAKE PARKER (#5-6)

COLOR ARTIST
JEAN-FRANÇOIS BEAULIEU

LETTERER: **JEFF ECKLEBERRY**
COVER ART: **SKOTTIE YOUNG**
ASSISTANT EDITOR: **DEVIN LEWIS**
EDITOR: **SANA AMANAT**
SENIOR EDITOR: **NICK LOWE**
SPECIAL THANKS TO **STEPHEN WACKER**

COLLECTION EDITOR: JENNIFER GRÜNWALD • ASSISTANT EDITOR: SARAH BRUNSTAD
ASSOCIATE MANAGING EDITOR: ALEX STARBUCK • EDITOR, SPECIAL PROJECTS: MARK D. BEAZLEY
SENIOR EDITOR, SPECIAL PROJECTS: JEFF YOUNGQUIST • SVP PRINT, SALES & MARKETING: DAVID GABRIEL
BOOK DESIGN: JEFF POWELL

EDITOR IN CHIEF: AXEL ALONSO • CHIEF CREATIVE OFFICER: JOE QUESADA • PUBLISHER: DAN BUCKLEY
EXECUTIVE PRODUCER: ALAN FINE

ROCKET RACCOON VOL. 1: A CHASING TALE. Contains material originally published in magazine form as ROCKET RACCOON #1-6. First printing 2015. ISBN# 978-0-7851-9389-0. Published by MARVEL WORLDWIDE, INC., a subsidiary of MARVEL ENTERTAINMENT, LLC. OFFICE OF PUBLICATION: 135 West 50th Street, New York, NY 10020. Copyright © 2014 and 2015 Marvel Characters, Inc. All rights reserved. All characters featured in this issue and the distinctive names and likenesses thereof, and all related indicia are trademarks of Marvel Characters, Inc. No similarity between any of the names, characters, persons, and/or institutions in this magazine with those of any living or dead person or institution is intended, and any such similarity which may exist is purely coincidental. **Printed in the U.S.A.** ALAN FINE, EVP - Office of the President, Marvel Worldwide, Inc. and EVP & CMO Marvel Characters B.V.; DAN BUCKLEY, Publisher & President - Print, Animation & Digital Divisions; JOE QUESADA, Chief Creative Officer; TOM BREVOORT, SVP of Publishing; DAVID BOGART, SVP of Operations & Procurement, Publishing; C.B. CEBULSKI, SVP of Creator & Content Development; DAVID GABRIEL, SVP Print, Sales & Marketing; JIM O'KEEFE, VP of Operations & Logistics; DAN CARR, Executive Director of Publishing Technology; SUSAN CRESPI, Editorial Operations Manager; ALEX MORALES, Publishing Operations Manager; STAN LEE, Chairman Emeritus. For information regarding advertising in Marvel Comics or on Marvel.com, please contact Niza Disla, Director of Marvel Partnerships, at ndisla@marvel.com. For Marvel subscription inquiries, please call 800-217-9158. **Manufactured between 12/12/2014 and 1/26/2015 by R.R. DONNELLEY, INC., SALEM, VA, USA.**

10 9 8 7 6 5 4 3 2 1

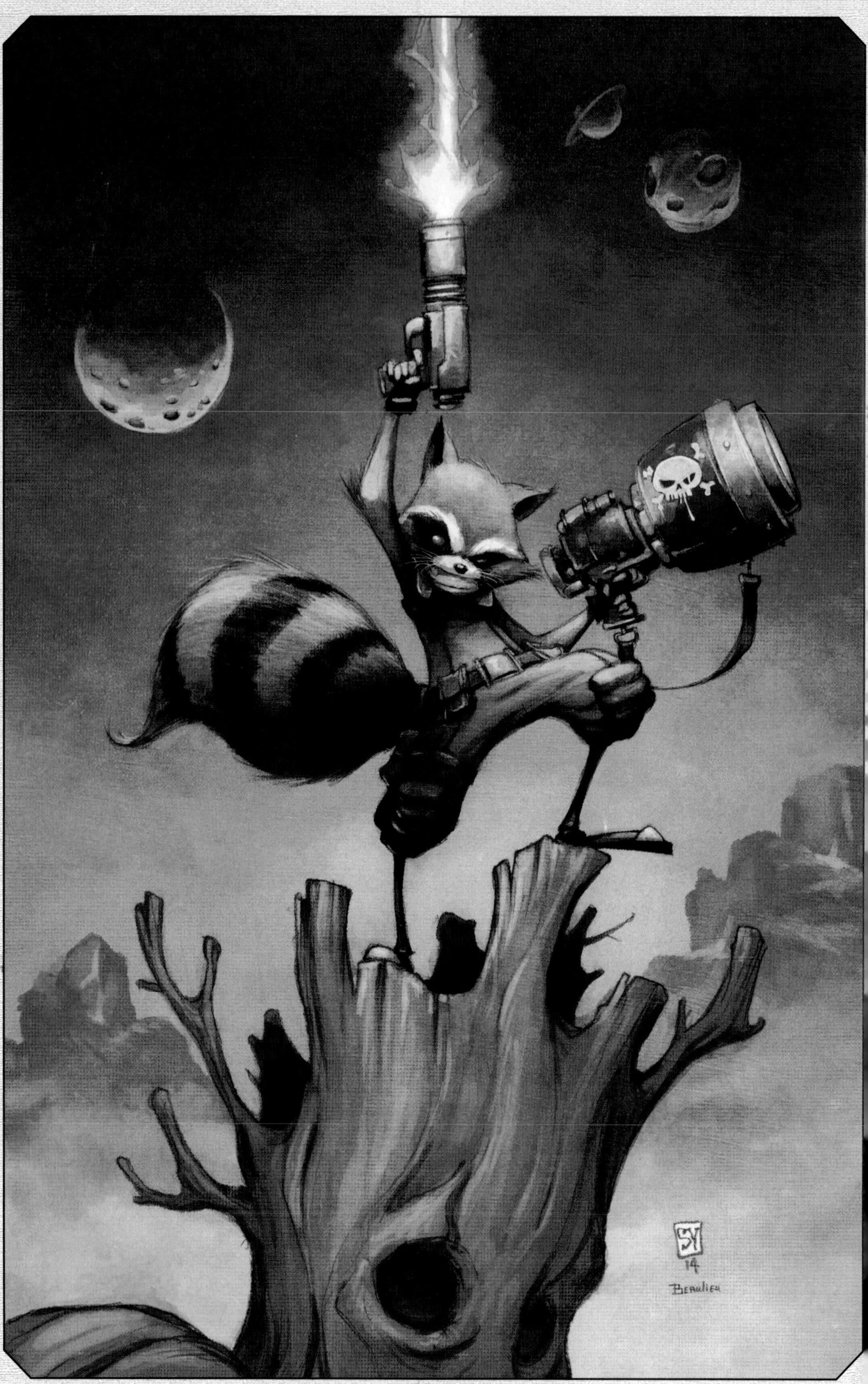
SY
14
Beaulieu

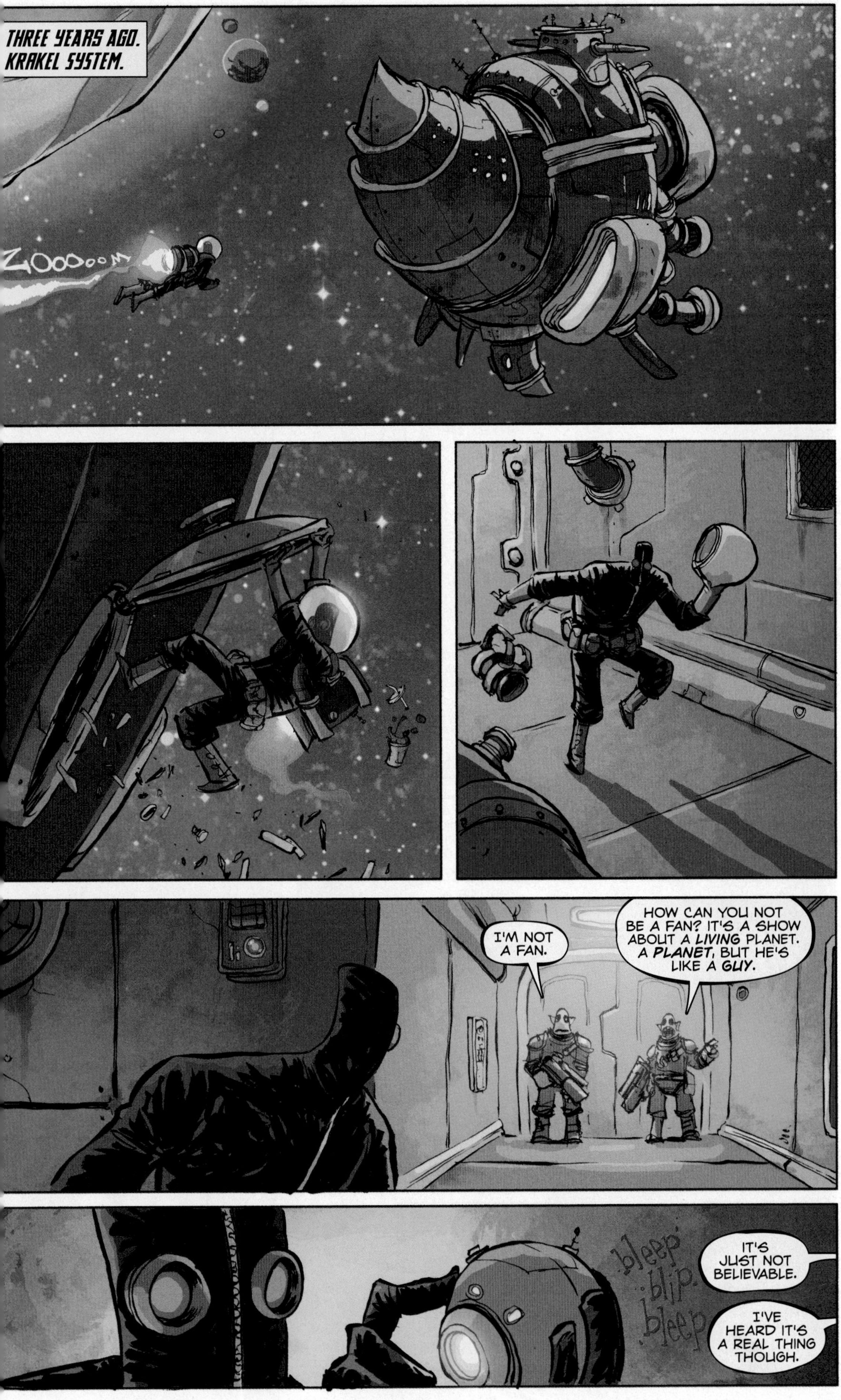
THREE YEARS AGO. KRAKEL SYSTEM.
ZOOOOOOM
I'M NOT A FAN.
HOW CAN YOU NOT BE A FAN? IT'S A SHOW ABOUT A LIVING PLANET. A PLANET, BUT HE'S LIKE A GUY.
bleep
blip
bleep
IT'S JUST NOT BELIEVABLE.
I'VE HEARD IT'S A REAL THING THOUGH.

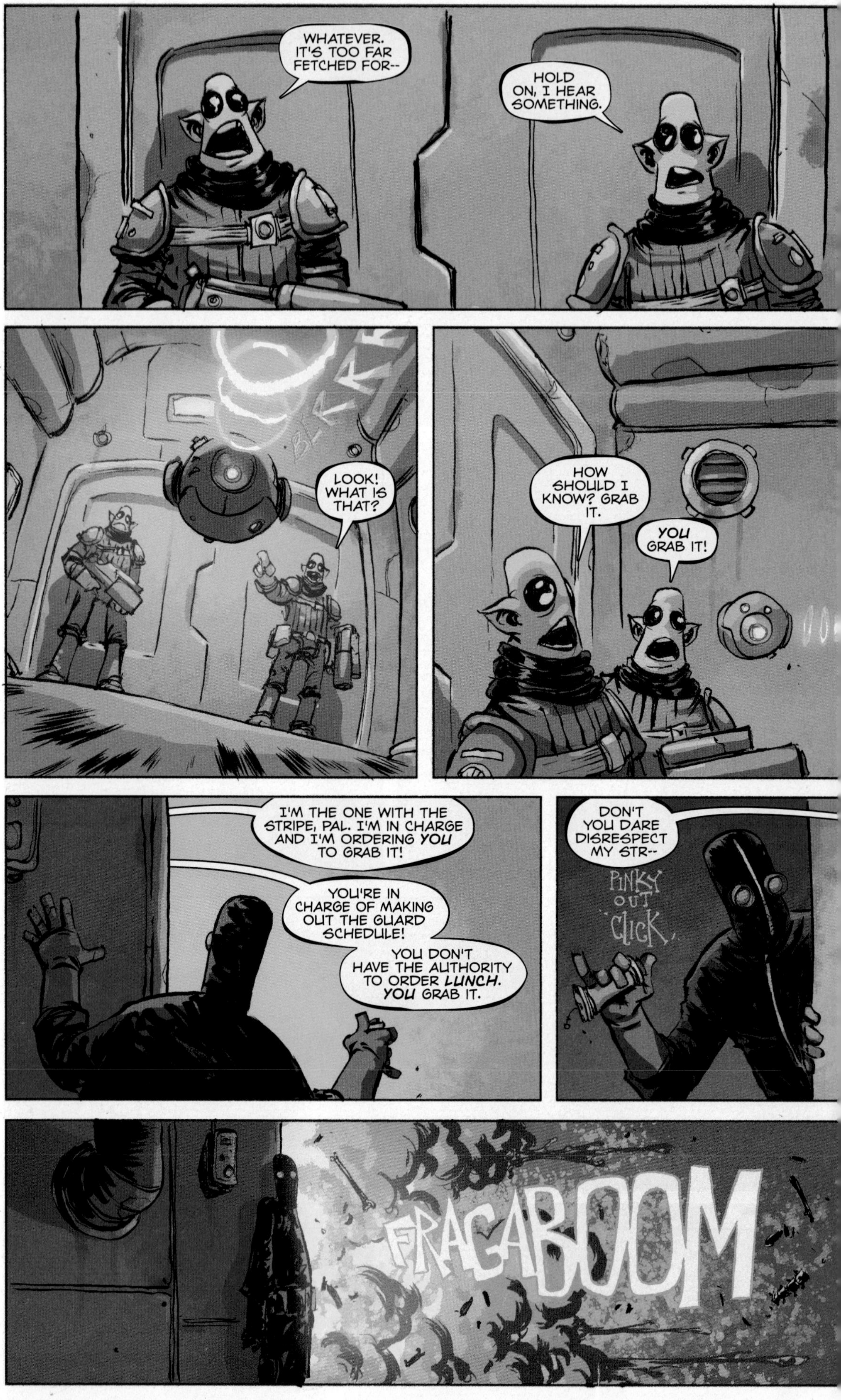

WHATEVER. IT'S TOO FAR FETCHED FOR--
HOLD ON, I HEAR SOMETHING.
BLRRR
LOOK! WHAT IS THAT?
HOW SHOULD I KNOW? GRAB IT.
YOU GRAB IT!
I'M THE ONE WITH THE STRIPE, PAL. I'M IN CHARGE AND I'M ORDERING YOU TO GRAB IT!
YOU'RE IN CHARGE OF MAKING OUT THE GUARD SCHEDULE!
YOU DON'T HAVE THE AUTHORITY TO ORDER LUNCH. YOU GRAB IT.
DON'T YOU DARE DISRESPECT MY STR--
PINKY OUT CLICK
FRAGABOOM

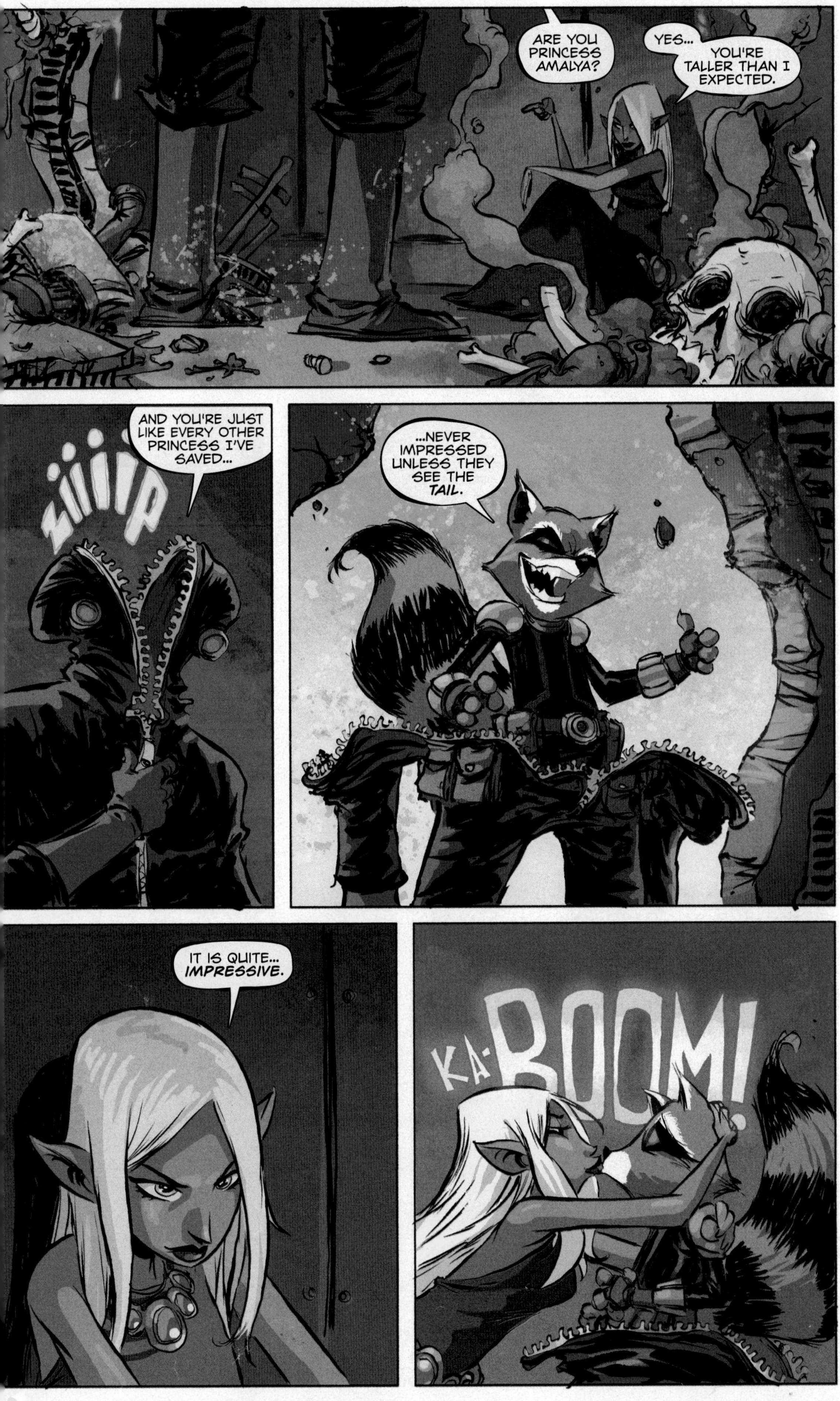
ARE YOU PRINCESS AMALYA?
YES...
YOU'RE TALLER THAN I EXPECTED.
AND YOU'RE JUST LIKE EVERY OTHER PRINCESS I'VE SAVED...
ZIIIIP
...NEVER IMPRESSED UNLESS THEY SEE THE *TAIL*.
IT IS QUITE... *IMPRESSIVE*.
KA-BOOM!

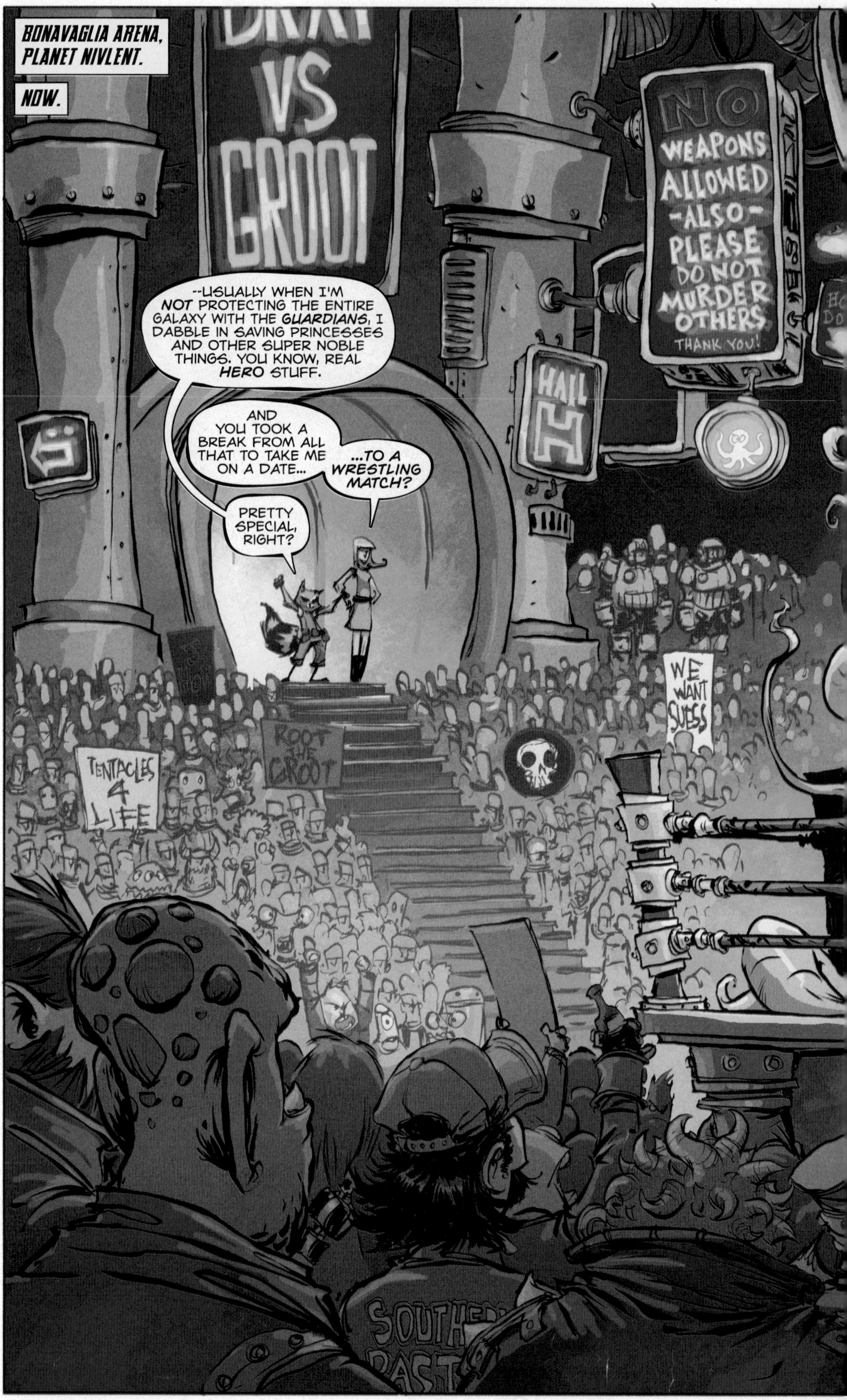
BONAVAGLIA ARENA, PLANET NIVLENT.
NOW.
VS GROOT
NO WEAPONS ALLOWED -ALSO- PLEASE DO NOT MURDER OTHERS THANK YOU!
HAIL H
--USUALLY WHEN I'M NOT PROTECTING THE ENTIRE GALAXY WITH THE GUARDIANS, I DABBLE IN SAVING PRINCESSES AND OTHER SUPER NOBLE THINGS. YOU KNOW, REAL HERO STUFF.
AND YOU TOOK A BREAK FROM ALL THAT TO TAKE ME ON A DATE...
...TO A WRESTLING MATCH?
PRETTY SPECIAL, RIGHT?
WE WANT SUESS
ROOT THE GROOT
TENTACLES 4 LIFE

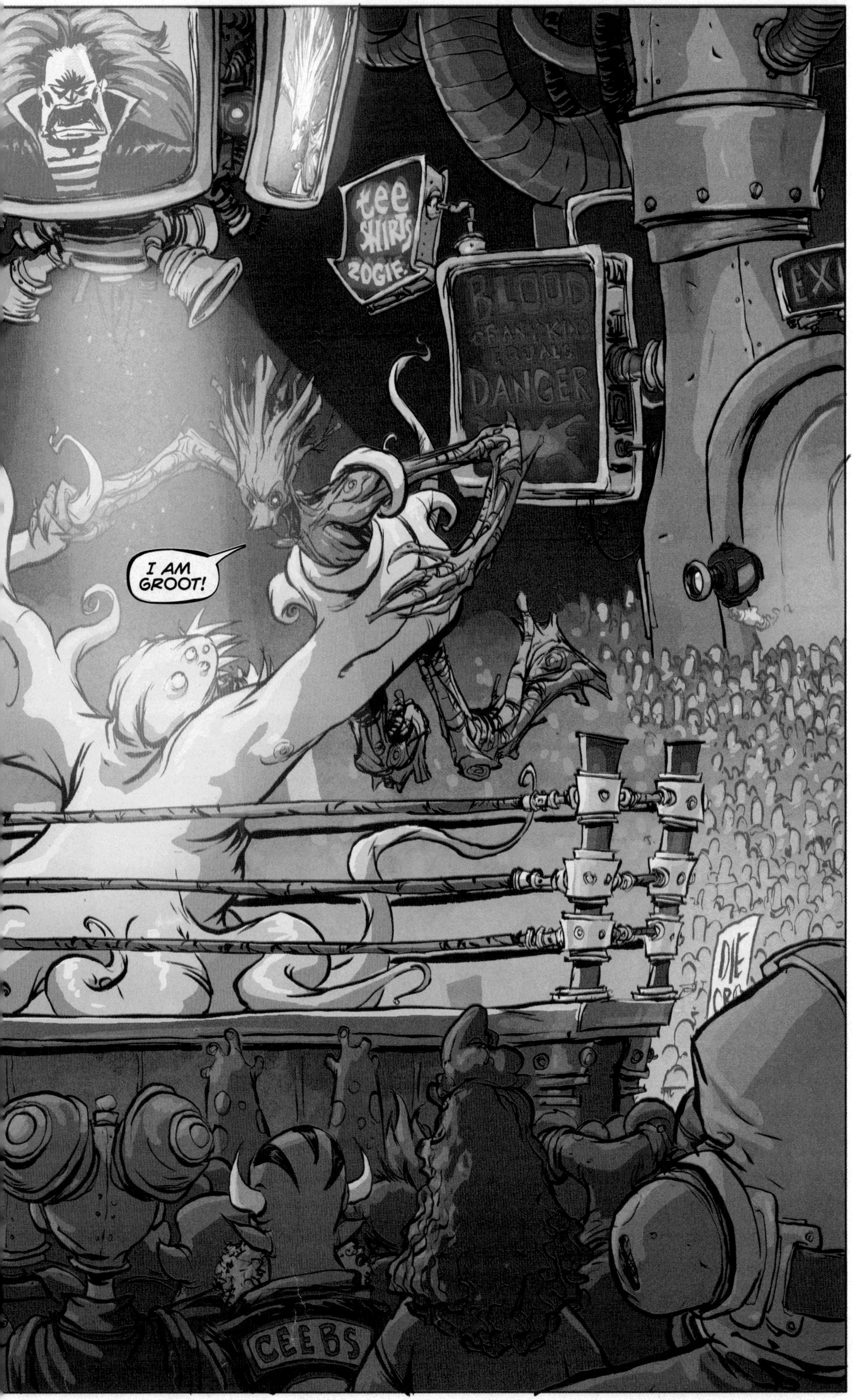
tee SHIRTS ZOGIE.
BLOOD
DANGER
I AM GROOT!
CEEBS

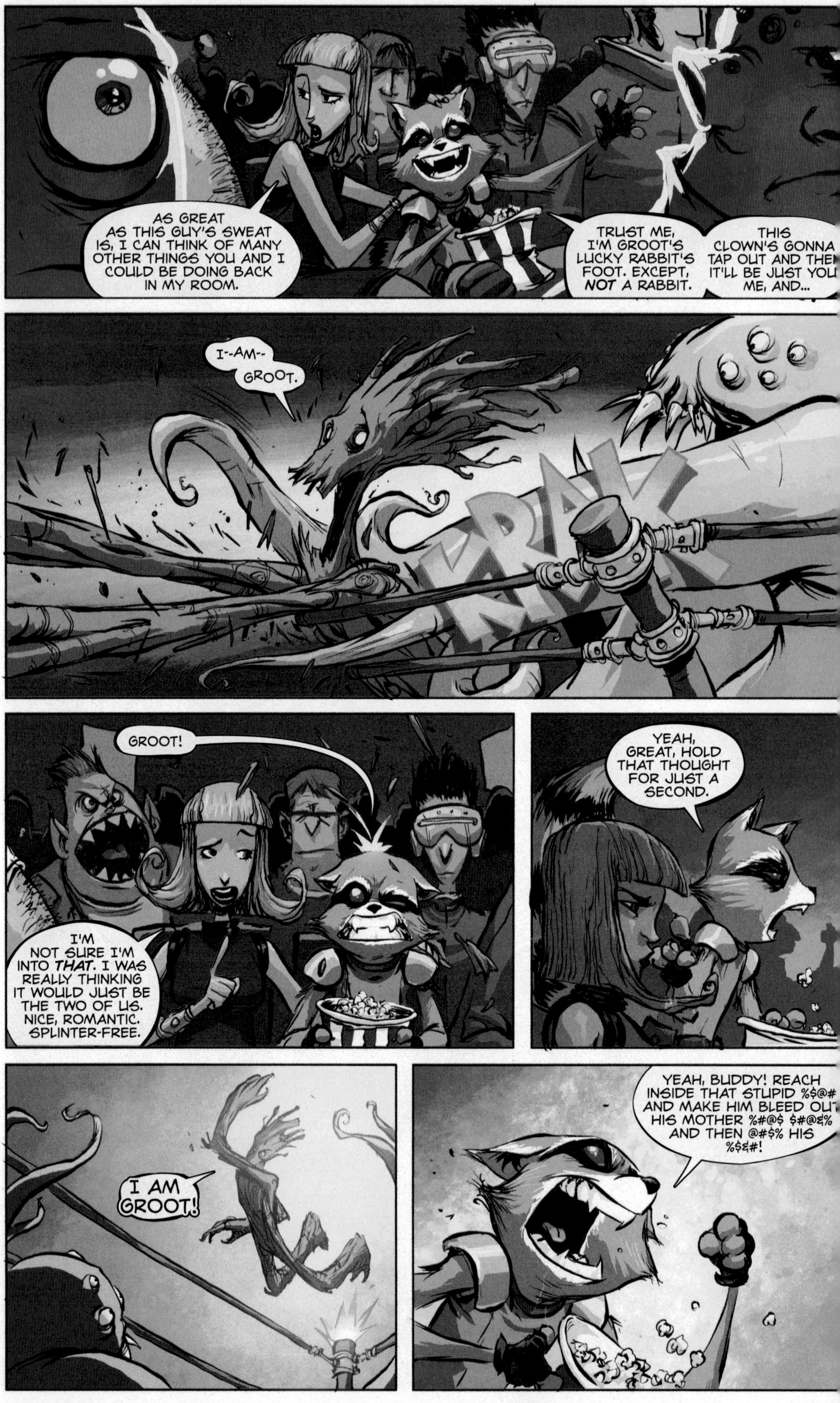
AS GREAT AS THIS GUY'S SWEAT IS, I CAN THINK OF MANY OTHER THINGS YOU AND I COULD BE DOING BACK IN MY ROOM.
TRUST ME, I'M GROOT'S LUCKY RABBIT'S FOOT. EXCEPT, NOT A RABBIT.
THIS CLOWN'S GONNA TAP OUT AND THEN IT'LL BE JUST YOU, ME, AND...
I--AM-- GROOT.
KRAK
GROOT!
I'M NOT SURE I'M INTO THAT. I WAS REALLY THINKING IT WOULD JUST BE THE TWO OF US. NICE, ROMANTIC. SPLINTER-FREE.
YEAH, GREAT, HOLD THAT THOUGHT FOR JUST A SECOND.
I AM GROOT!
YEAH, BUDDY! REACH INSIDE THAT STUPID %$@# AND MAKE HIM BLEED OUT HIS MOTHER %#@$ $#@&% AND THEN @#$% HIS %$&#!

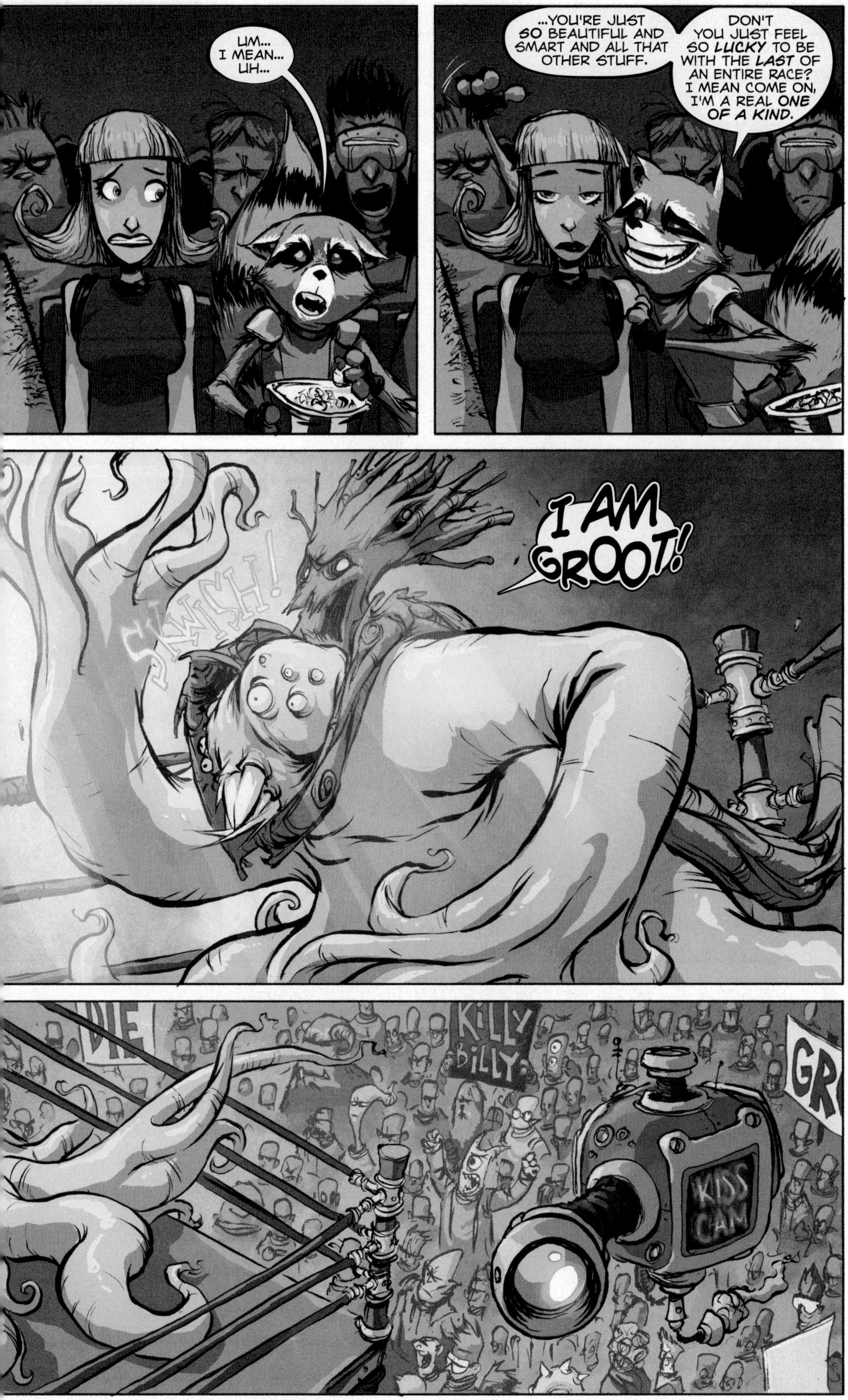

UM... I MEAN... UH...
...YOU'RE JUST SO BEAUTIFUL AND SMART AND ALL THAT OTHER STUFF.
DON'T YOU JUST FEEL SO LUCKY TO BE WITH THE LAST OF AN ENTIRE RACE? I MEAN COME ON, I'M A REAL ONE OF A KIND.
SWISH!
I AM GROOT!
DIE
KILLY BILLY
GR
KISS CAM

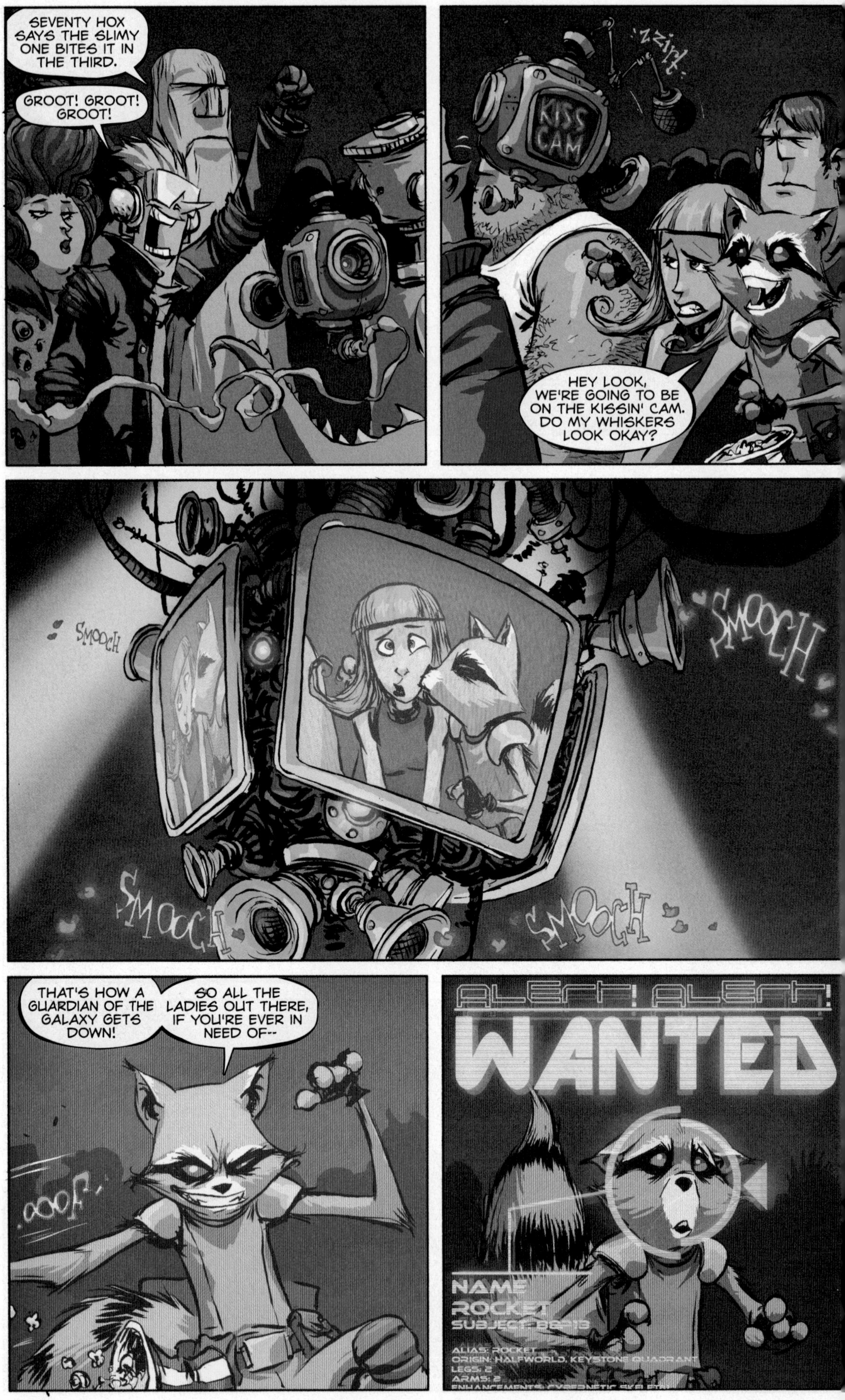
SEVENTY HOX SAYS THE SLIMY ONE BITES IT IN THE THIRD.
GROOT! GROOT! GROOT!
KISS CAM
ZZIRT
HEY LOOK, WE'RE GOING TO BE ON THE KISSIN' CAM. DO MY WHISKERS LOOK OKAY?
SMOOCH
SMOOCH
SMOOCH
SMOOCH
THAT'S HOW A GUARDIAN OF THE GALAXY GETS DOWN!
SO ALL THE LADIES OUT THERE, IF YOU'RE EVER IN NEED OF--
OOOF!
ALERT! ALERT!
WANTED
NAME
ROCKET
SUBJECT 89P13
ALIAS: ROCKET
ORIGIN: HALFWORLD, KEYSTONE QUADRANT
LEGS: 2
ARMS: 2

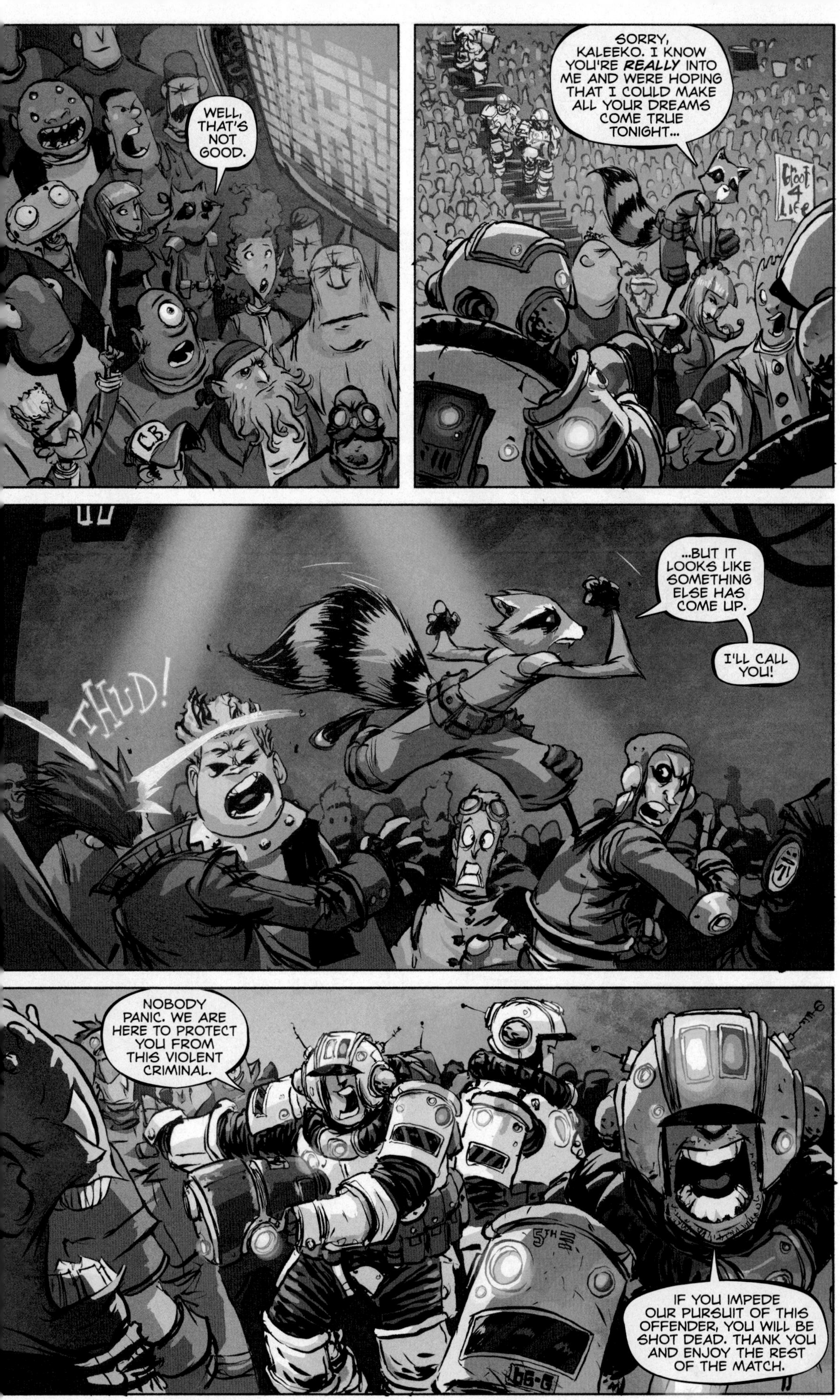
WELL, THAT'S NOT GOOD.
SORRY, KALEEKO. I KNOW YOU'RE *REALLY* INTO ME AND WERE HOPING THAT I COULD MAKE ALL YOUR DREAMS COME TRUE TONIGHT...
Groot 4 Life
...BUT IT LOOKS LIKE SOMETHING ELSE HAS COME UP.
I'LL CALL YOU!
THUD!
NOBODY PANIC. WE ARE HERE TO PROTECT YOU FROM THIS VIOLENT CRIMINAL.
IF YOU IMPEDE OUR PURSUIT OF THIS OFFENDER, YOU WILL BE SHOT DEAD. THANK YOU AND ENJOY THE REST OF THE MATCH.

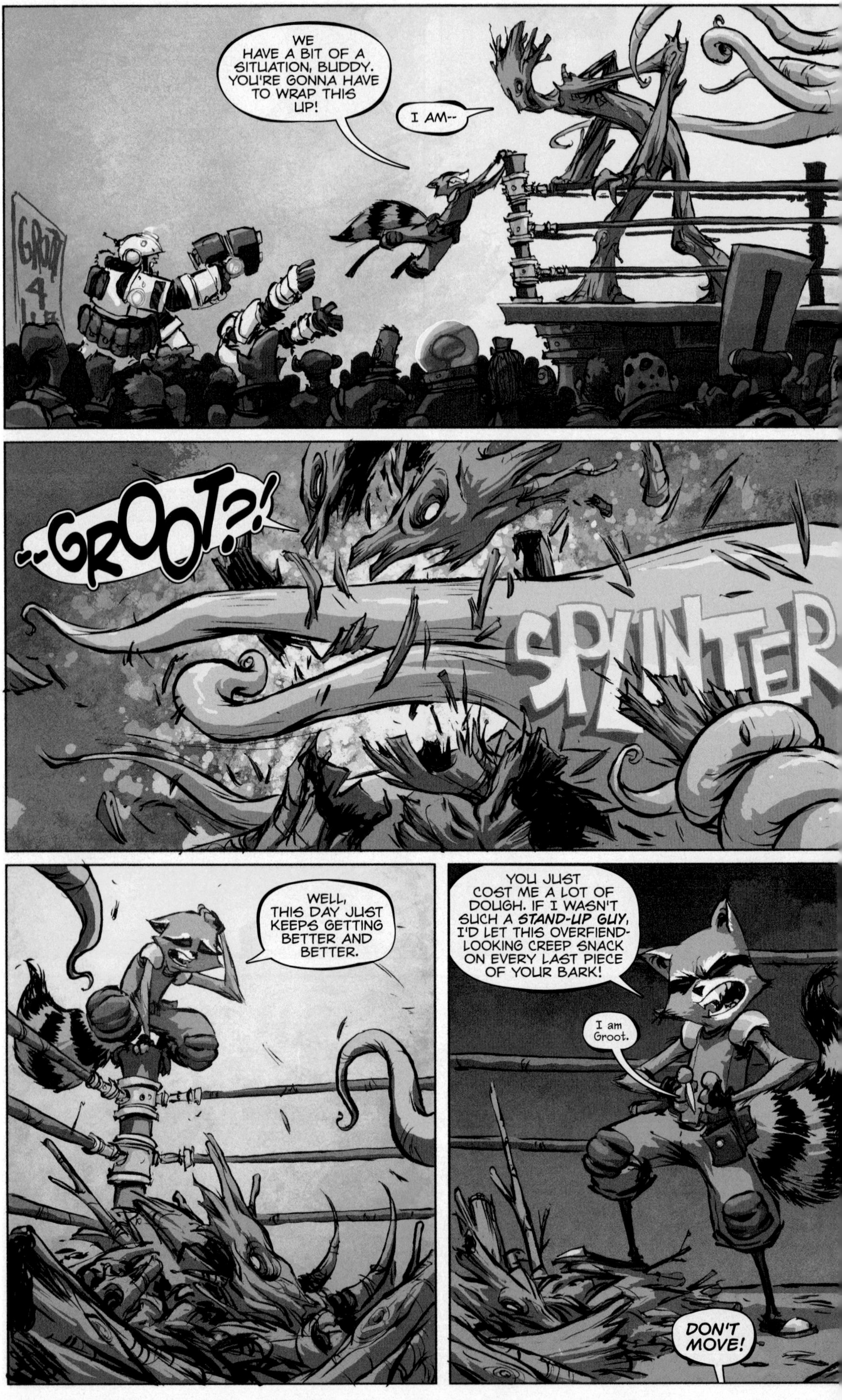

WE HAVE A BIT OF A SITUATION, BUDDY. YOU'RE GONNA HAVE TO WRAP THIS UP!
I AM--
--GROOT?!
SPLINTER
WELL, THIS DAY JUST KEEPS GETTING BETTER AND BETTER.
YOU JUST COST ME A LOT OF DOUGH. IF I WASN'T SUCH A STAND-UP GUY, I'D LET THIS OVERFIEND-LOOKING CREEP SNACK ON EVERY LAST PIECE OF YOUR BARK!
I am Groot.
DON'T MOVE!

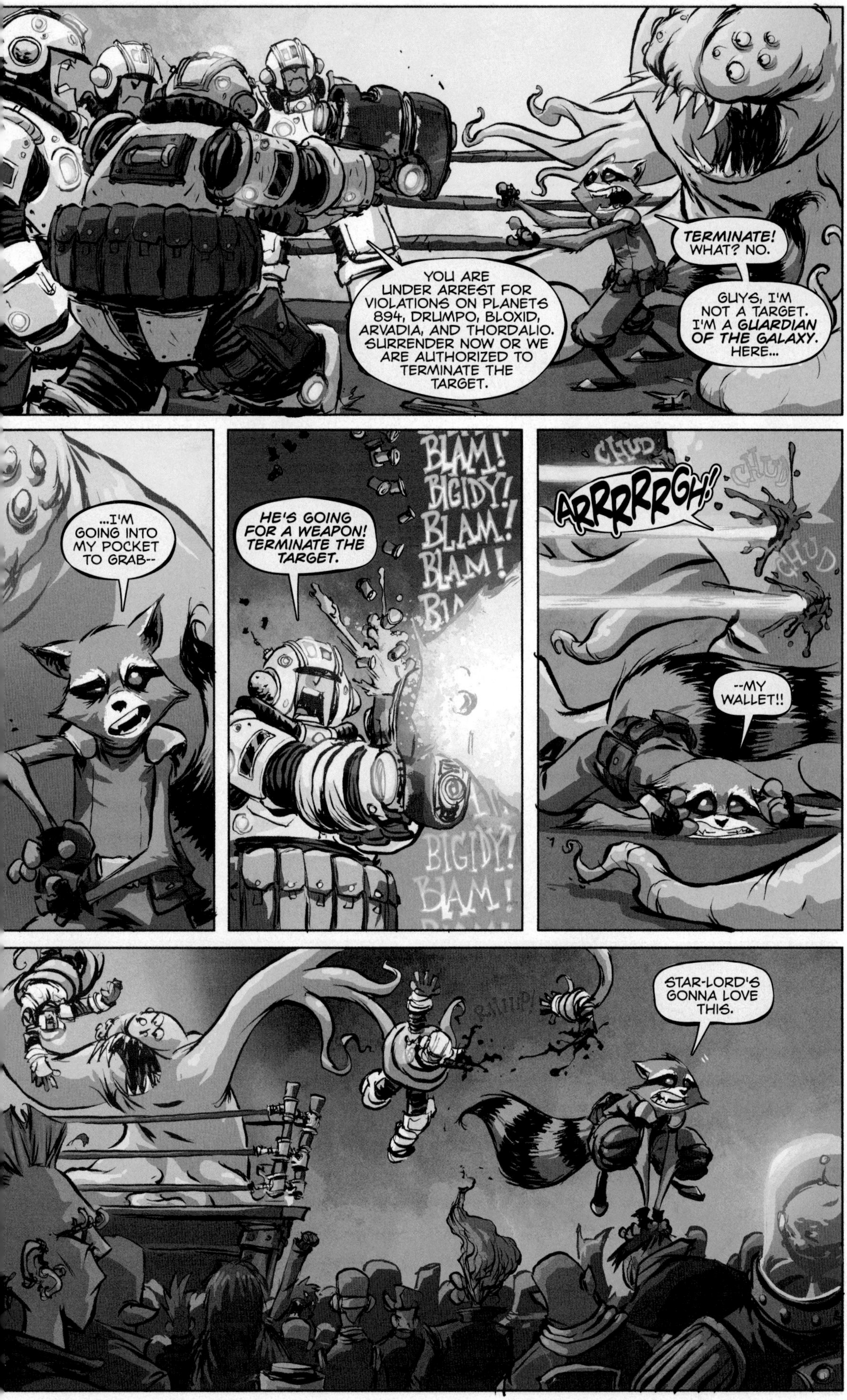
YOU ARE UNDER ARREST FOR VIOLATIONS ON PLANETS 894, DRUMPO, BLOXID, ARVADIA, AND THORDALIO. SURRENDER NOW OR WE ARE AUTHORIZED TO TERMINATE THE TARGET.
TERMINATE! WHAT? NO.
GUYS, I'M NOT A TARGET. I'M A GUARDIAN OF THE GALAXY. HERE...
...I'M GOING INTO MY POCKET TO GRAB--
HE'S GOING FOR A WEAPON! TERMINATE THE TARGET.
BLAM! BIGIDY! BLAM! BLAM!
BIGIDY! BLAM!
CHUD
ARRRRRGH!
CHUD
CHUD
--MY WALLET!!
STAR-LORD'S GONNA LOVE THIS.

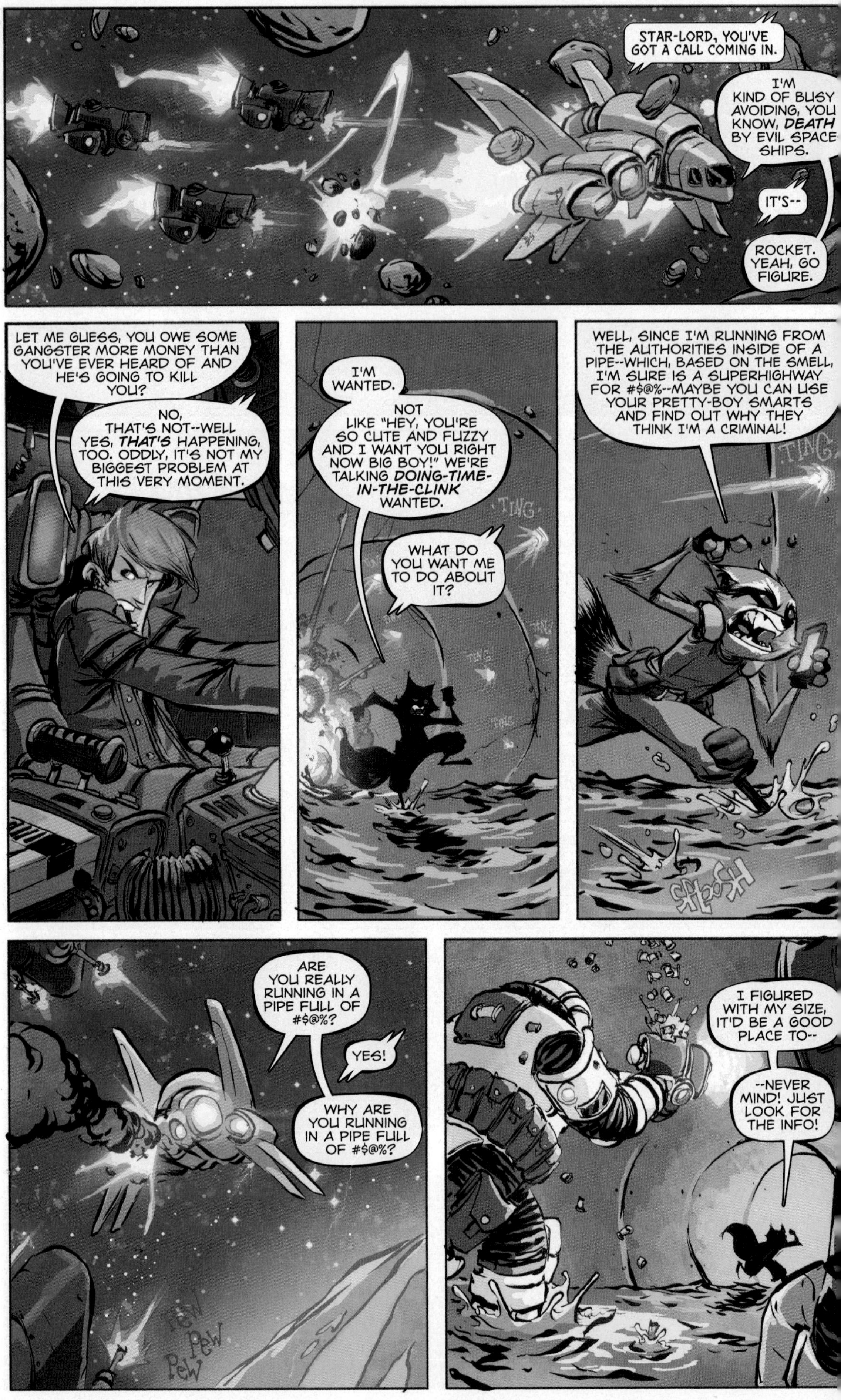
STAR-LORD, YOU'VE GOT A CALL COMING IN.
I'M KIND OF BUSY AVOIDING, YOU KNOW, *DEATH* BY EVIL SPACE SHIPS.
IT'S--
ROCKET. YEAH, GO FIGURE.
LET ME GUESS, YOU OWE SOME GANGSTER MORE MONEY THAN YOU'VE EVER HEARD OF AND HE'S GOING TO KILL YOU?
NO, THAT'S NOT--WELL YES, *THAT'S* HAPPENING, TOO. ODDLY, IT'S NOT MY BIGGEST PROBLEM AT THIS VERY MOMENT.
I'M WANTED.
NOT LIKE "HEY, YOU'RE SO CUTE AND FUZZY AND I WANT YOU RIGHT NOW BIG BOY!" WE'RE TALKING *DOING-TIME-IN-THE-CLINK* WANTED.
TING
WHAT DO YOU WANT ME TO DO ABOUT IT?
WELL, SINCE I'M RUNNING FROM THE AUTHORITIES INSIDE OF A PIPE--WHICH, BASED ON THE SMELL, I'M SURE IS A SUPERHIGHWAY FOR #$@%--MAYBE YOU CAN USE YOUR PRETTY-BOY SMARTS AND FIND OUT WHY THEY THINK I'M A CRIMINAL!
TING
ARE YOU REALLY RUNNING IN A PIPE FULL OF #$@%?
YES!
WHY ARE YOU RUNNING IN A PIPE FULL OF #$@%?
PEW PEW PEW
I FIGURED WITH MY SIZE, IT'D BE A GOOD PLACE TO--
--NEVER MIND! JUST LOOK FOR THE INFO!

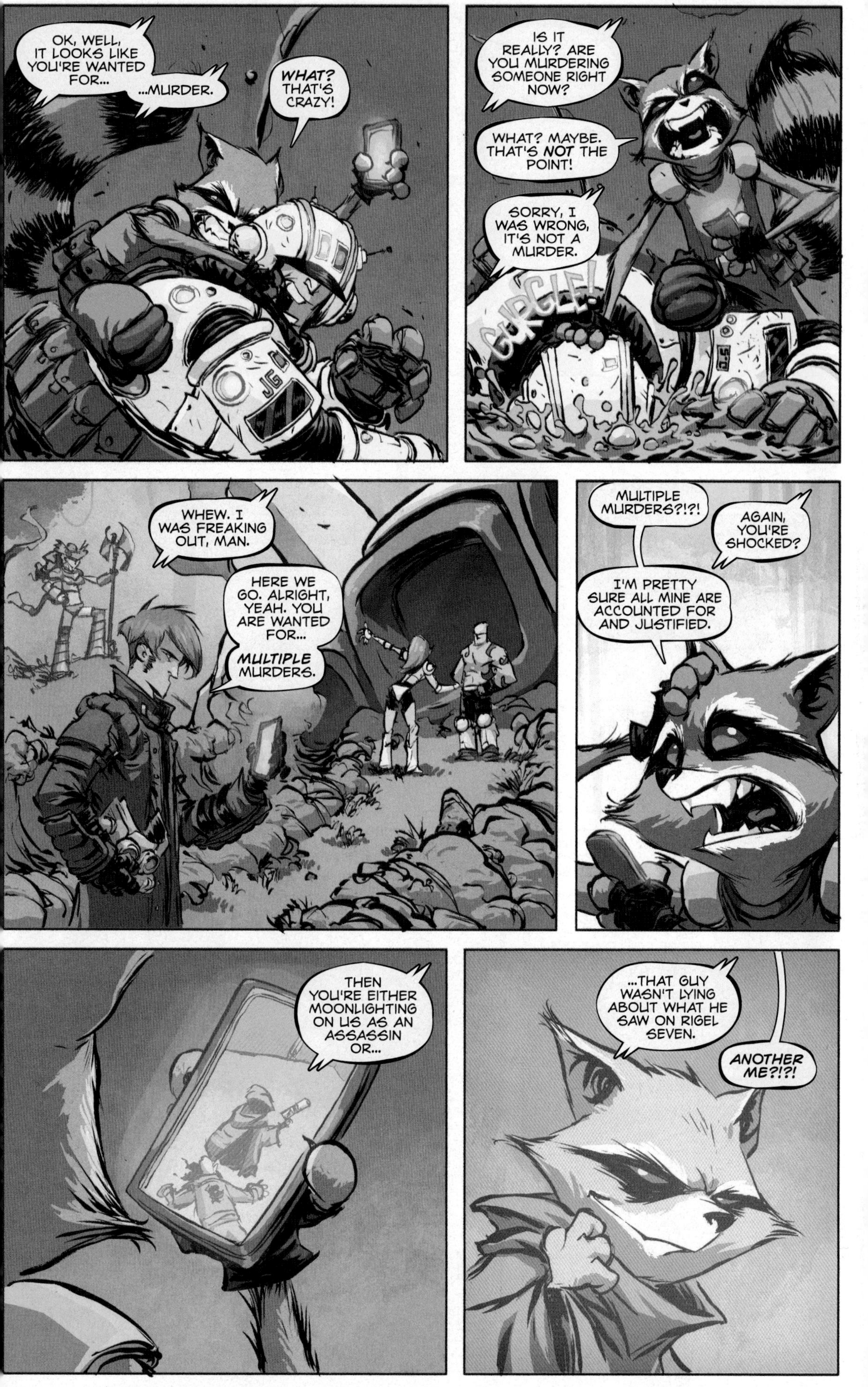
OK, WELL, IT LOOKS LIKE YOU'RE WANTED FOR...
...MURDER.
WHAT? THAT'S CRAZY!
IS IT REALLY? ARE YOU MURDERING SOMEONE RIGHT NOW?
WHAT? MAYBE. THAT'S *NOT* THE POINT!
SORRY, I WAS WRONG, IT'S NOT A MURDER.
GURGLE!
WHEW. I WAS FREAKING OUT, MAN.
HERE WE GO. ALRIGHT, YEAH. YOU ARE WANTED FOR...
MULTIPLE MURDERS.
MULTIPLE MURDERS?!?!
AGAIN, YOU'RE SHOCKED?
I'M PRETTY SURE ALL MINE ARE ACCOUNTED FOR AND JUSTIFIED.
THEN YOU'RE EITHER MOONLIGHTING ON US AS AN ASSASSIN OR...
...THAT GUY WASN'T LYING ABOUT WHAT HE SAW ON RIGEL SEVEN.
ANOTHER ME?!?!

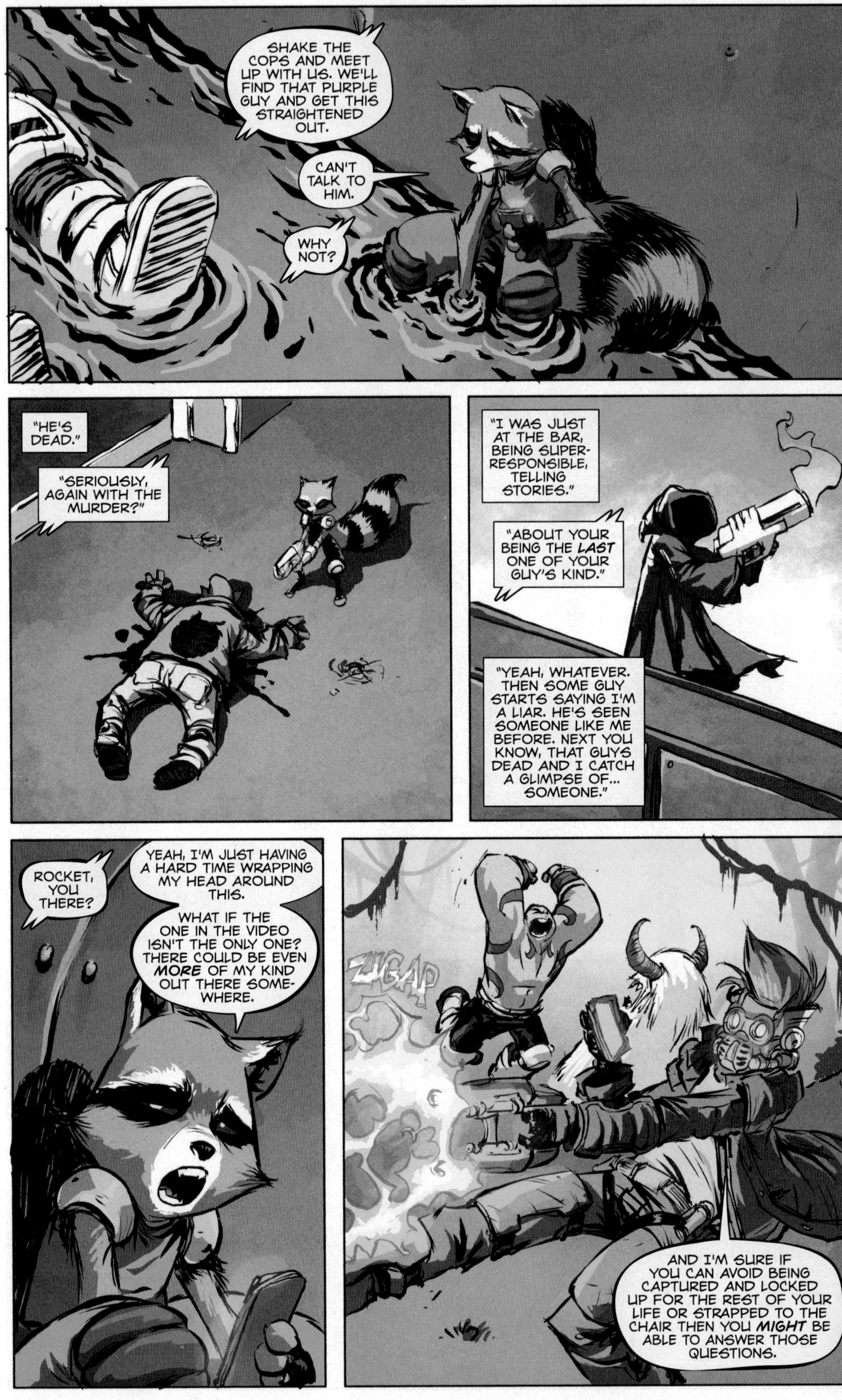
SHAKE THE COPS AND MEET UP WITH US. WE'LL FIND THAT PURPLE GUY AND GET THIS STRAIGHTENED OUT.
CAN'T TALK TO HIM.
WHY NOT?
"HE'S DEAD."
"SERIOUSLY, AGAIN WITH THE MURDER?"
"I WAS JUST AT THE BAR, BEING SUPER-RESPONSIBLE, TELLING STORIES."
"ABOUT YOUR BEING THE *LAST* ONE OF YOUR GUY'S KIND."
"YEAH, WHATEVER. THEN SOME GUY STARTS SAYING I'M A LIAR. HE'S SEEN SOMEONE LIKE ME BEFORE. NEXT YOU KNOW, THAT GUYS DEAD AND I CATCH A GLIMPSE OF... SOMEONE."
ROCKET, YOU THERE?
YEAH, I'M JUST HAVING A HARD TIME WRAPPING MY HEAD AROUND THIS.
WHAT IF THE ONE IN THE VIDEO ISN'T THE ONLY ONE? THERE COULD BE EVEN *MORE* OF MY KIND OUT THERE SOME-WHERE.
ZAGAP
AND I'M SURE IF YOU CAN AVOID BEING CAPTURED AND LOCKED UP FOR THE REST OF YOUR LIFE OR STRAPPED TO THE CHAIR THEN YOU *MIGHT* BE ABLE TO ANSWER THOSE QUESTIONS.

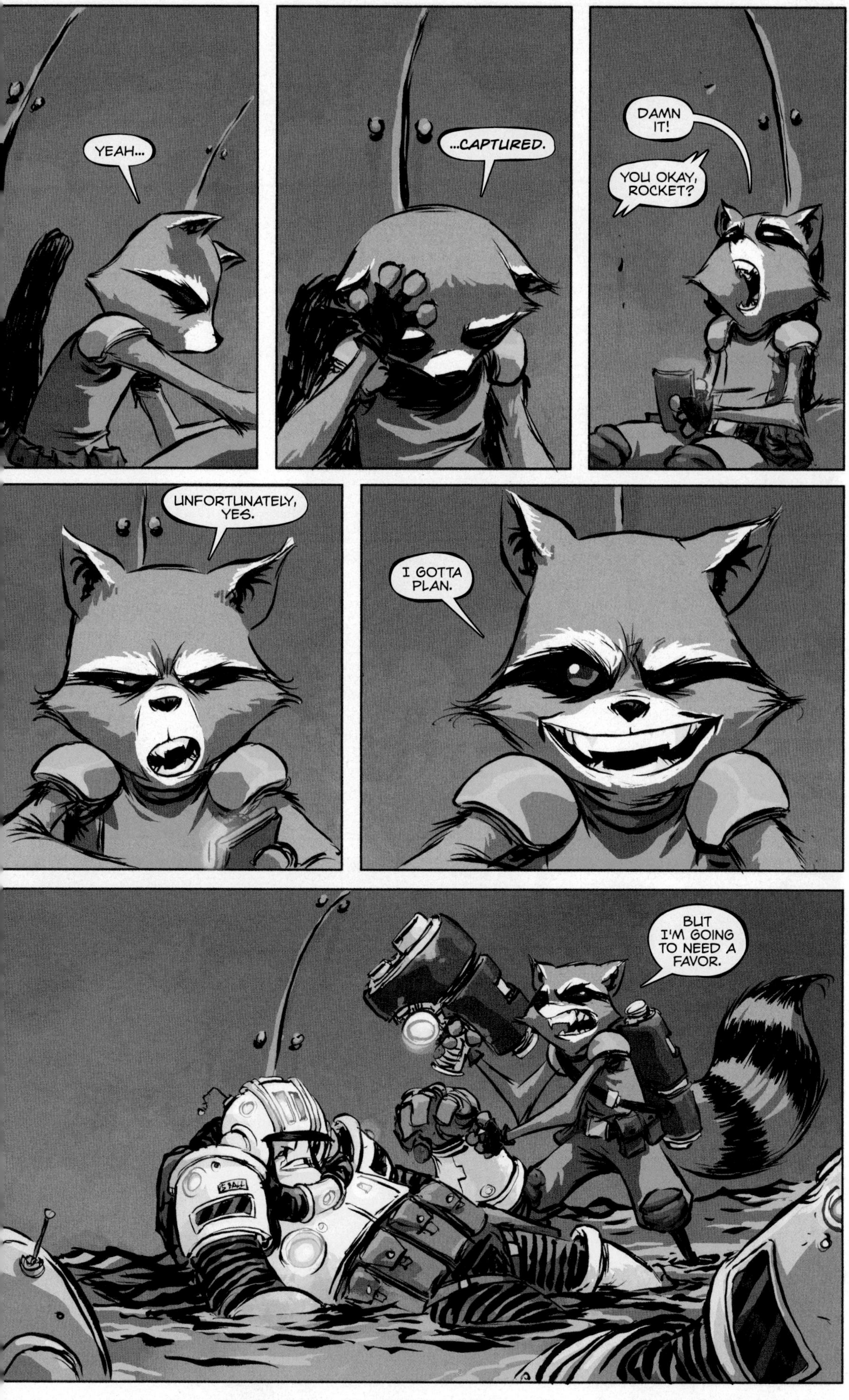
YEAH...
...CAPTURED.
DAMN IT!
YOU OKAY, ROCKET?
UNFORTUNATELY, YES.
I GOTTA PLAN.
BUT I'M GOING TO NEED A FAVOR.

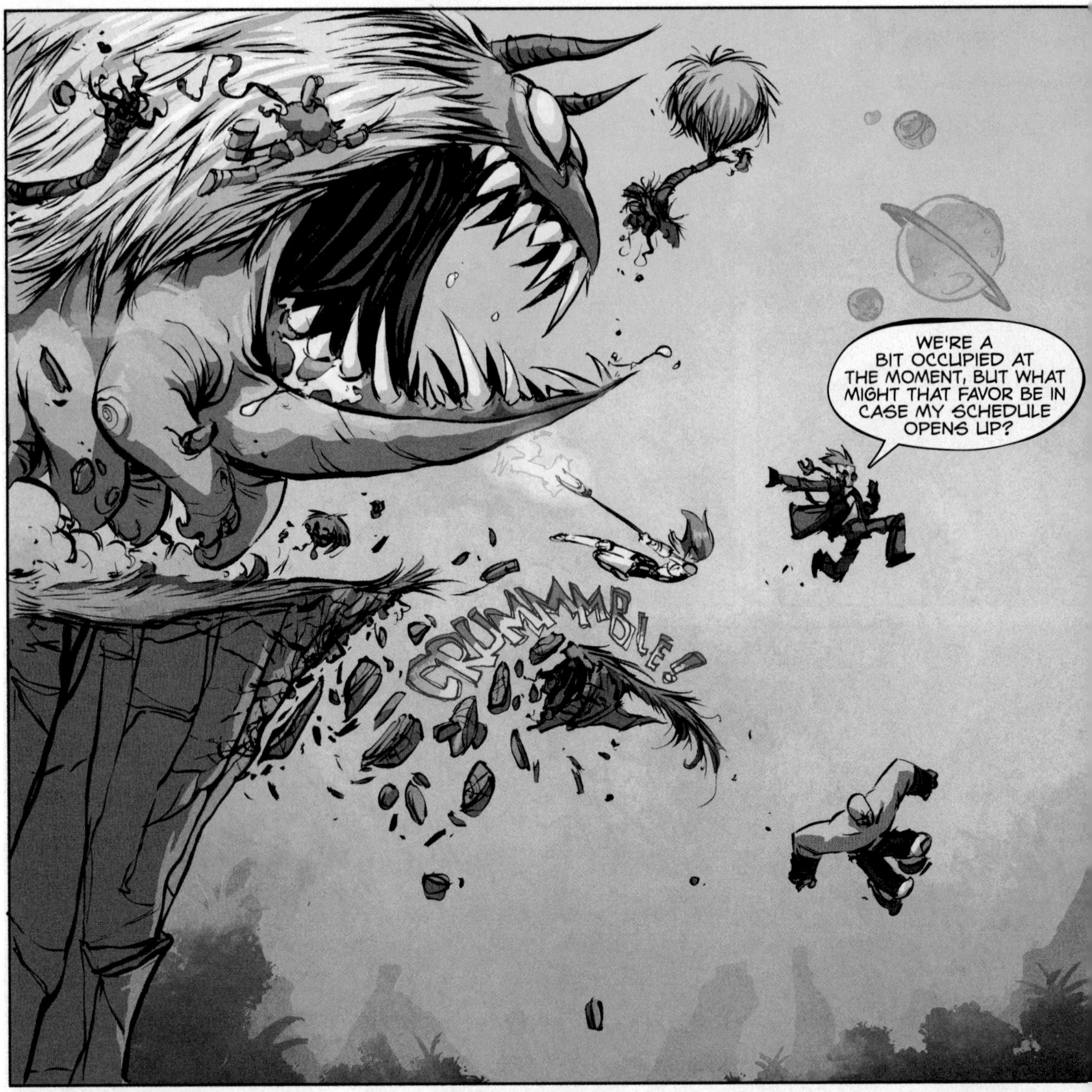
WE'RE A BIT OCCUPIED AT THE MOMENT, BUT WHAT MIGHT THAT FAVOR BE IN CASE MY SCHEDULE OPENS UP?
CRUMMMMBLE!

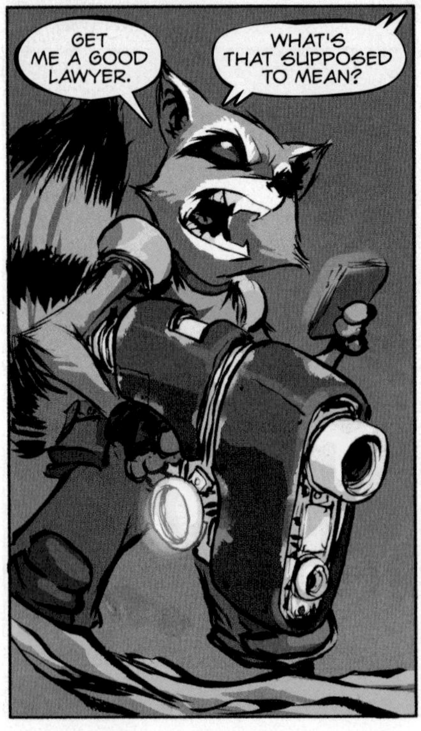
GET ME A GOOD LAWYER.
WHAT'S THAT SUPPOSED TO MEAN?

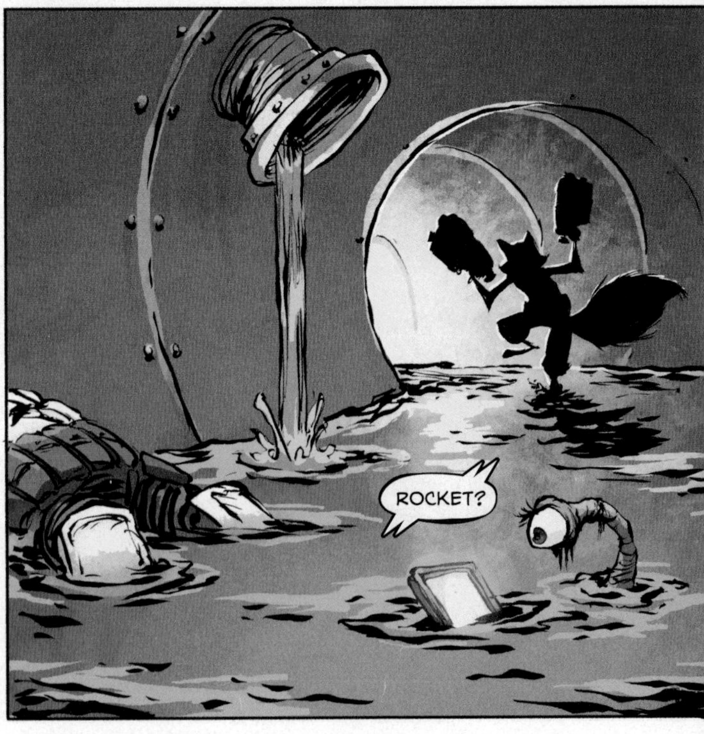
ROCKET?

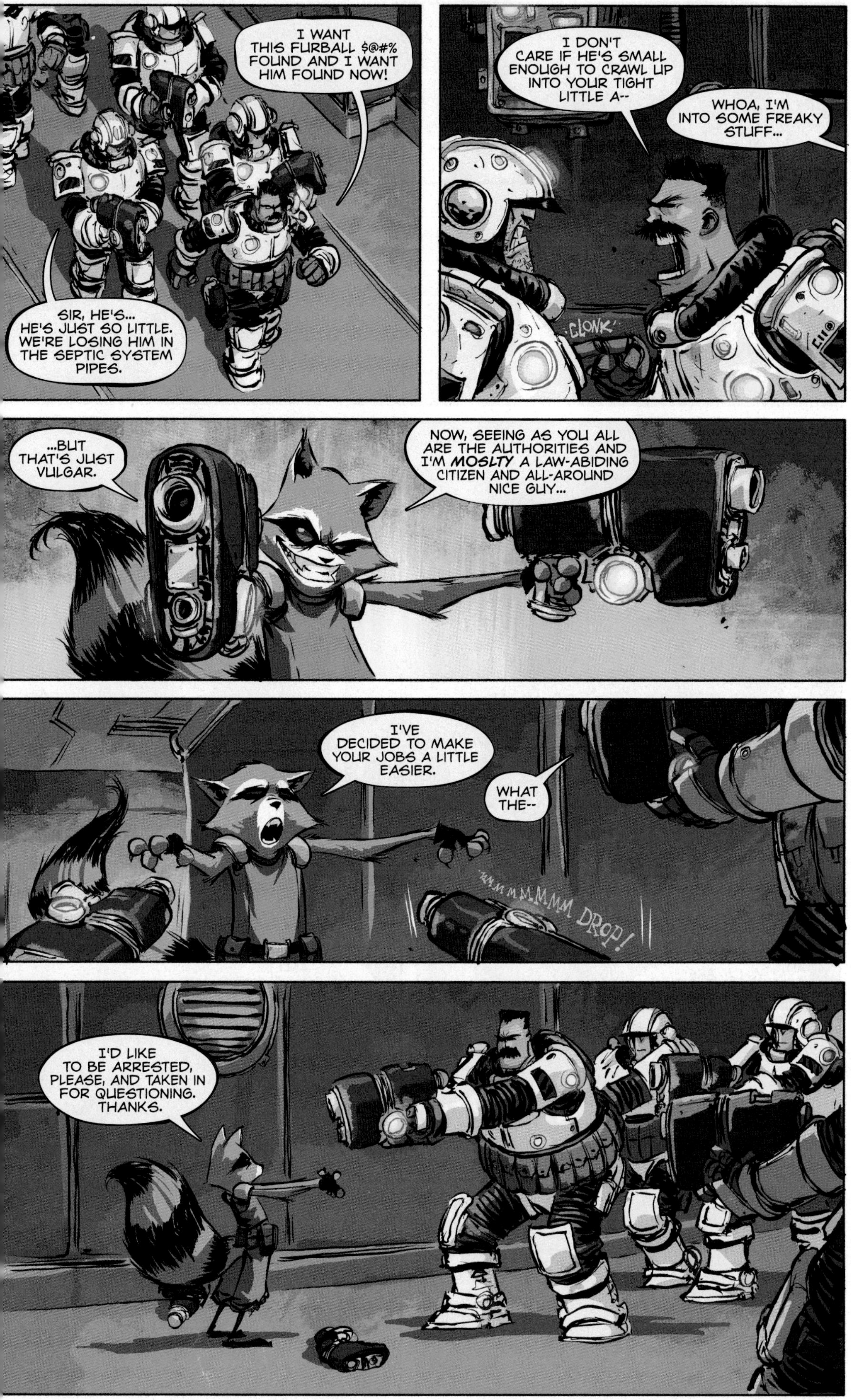
I WANT THIS FURBALL $@#% FOUND AND I WANT HIM FOUND NOW!
SIR, HE'S... HE'S JUST SO LITTLE. WE'RE LOSING HIM IN THE SEPTIC SYSTEM PIPES.
I DON'T CARE IF HE'S SMALL ENOUGH TO CRAWL UP INTO YOUR TIGHT LITTLE A--
WHOA, I'M INTO SOME FREAKY STUFF...
CLONK
...BUT THAT'S JUST VULGAR.
NOW, SEEING AS YOU ALL ARE THE AUTHORITIES AND I'M MOSLTY A LAW-ABIDING CITIZEN AND ALL-AROUND NICE GUY...
I'VE DECIDED TO MAKE YOUR JOBS A LITTLE EASIER.
WHAT THE--
MMMMMMMM DROP!
I'D LIKE TO BE ARRESTED, PLEASE, AND TAKEN IN FOR QUESTIONING. THANKS.

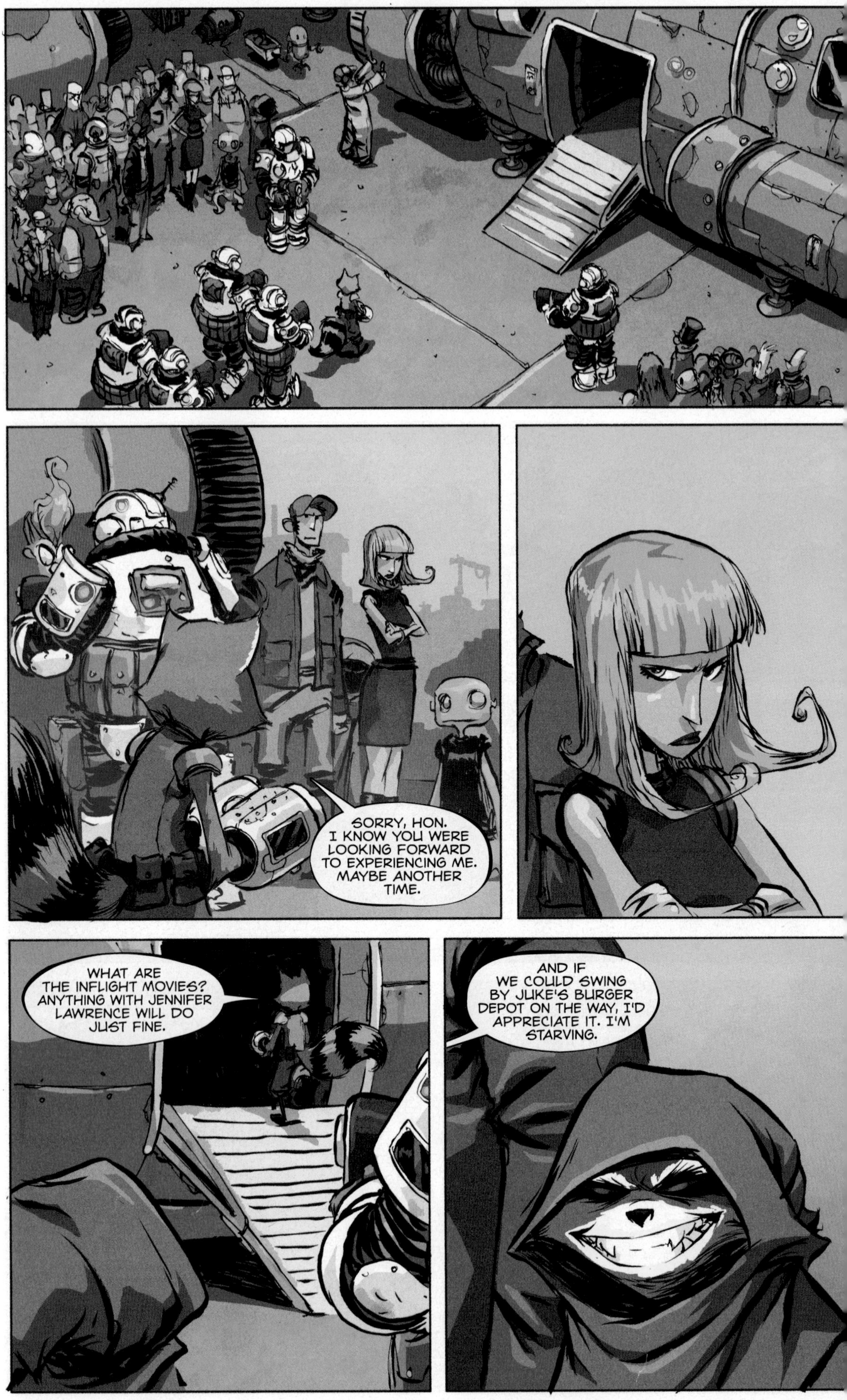
SORRY, HON. I KNOW YOU WERE LOOKING FORWARD TO EXPERIENCING ME. MAYBE ANOTHER TIME.
WHAT ARE THE INFLIGHT MOVIES? ANYTHING WITH JENNIFER LAWRENCE WILL DO JUST FINE.
AND IF WE COULD SWING BY JUKE'S BURGER DEPOT ON THE WAY, I'D APPRECIATE IT. I'M STARVING.

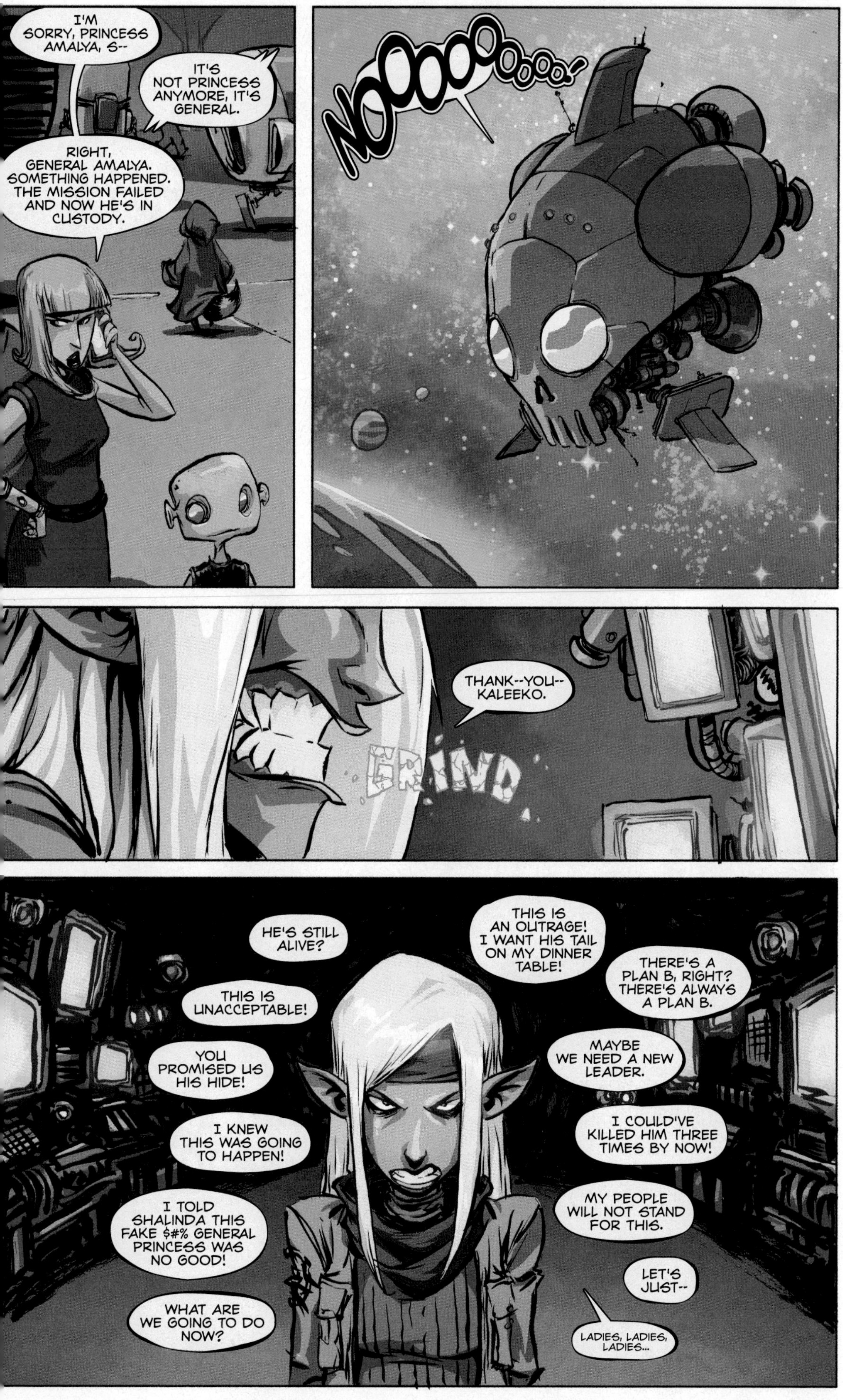
I'M SORRY, PRINCESS AMALYA, S--
IT'S NOT PRINCESS ANYMORE, IT'S GENERAL.
RIGHT, GENERAL AMALYA. SOMETHING HAPPENED. THE MISSION FAILED AND NOW HE'S IN CUSTODY.
NOOOOOoooo!
THANK--YOU--KALEEKO.
GRIND
HE'S STILL ALIVE?
THIS IS AN OUTRAGE! I WANT HIS TAIL ON MY DINNER TABLE!
THERE'S A PLAN B, RIGHT? THERE'S ALWAYS A PLAN B.
THIS IS UNACCEPTABLE!
MAYBE WE NEED A NEW LEADER.
YOU PROMISED US HIS HIDE!
I KNEW THIS WAS GOING TO HAPPEN!
I COULD'VE KILLED HIM THREE TIMES BY NOW!
I TOLD SHALINDA THIS FAKE $#% GENERAL PRINCESS WAS NO GOOD!
MY PEOPLE WILL NOT STAND FOR THIS.
LET'S JUST--
WHAT ARE WE GOING TO DO NOW?
LADIES, LADIES, LADIES...

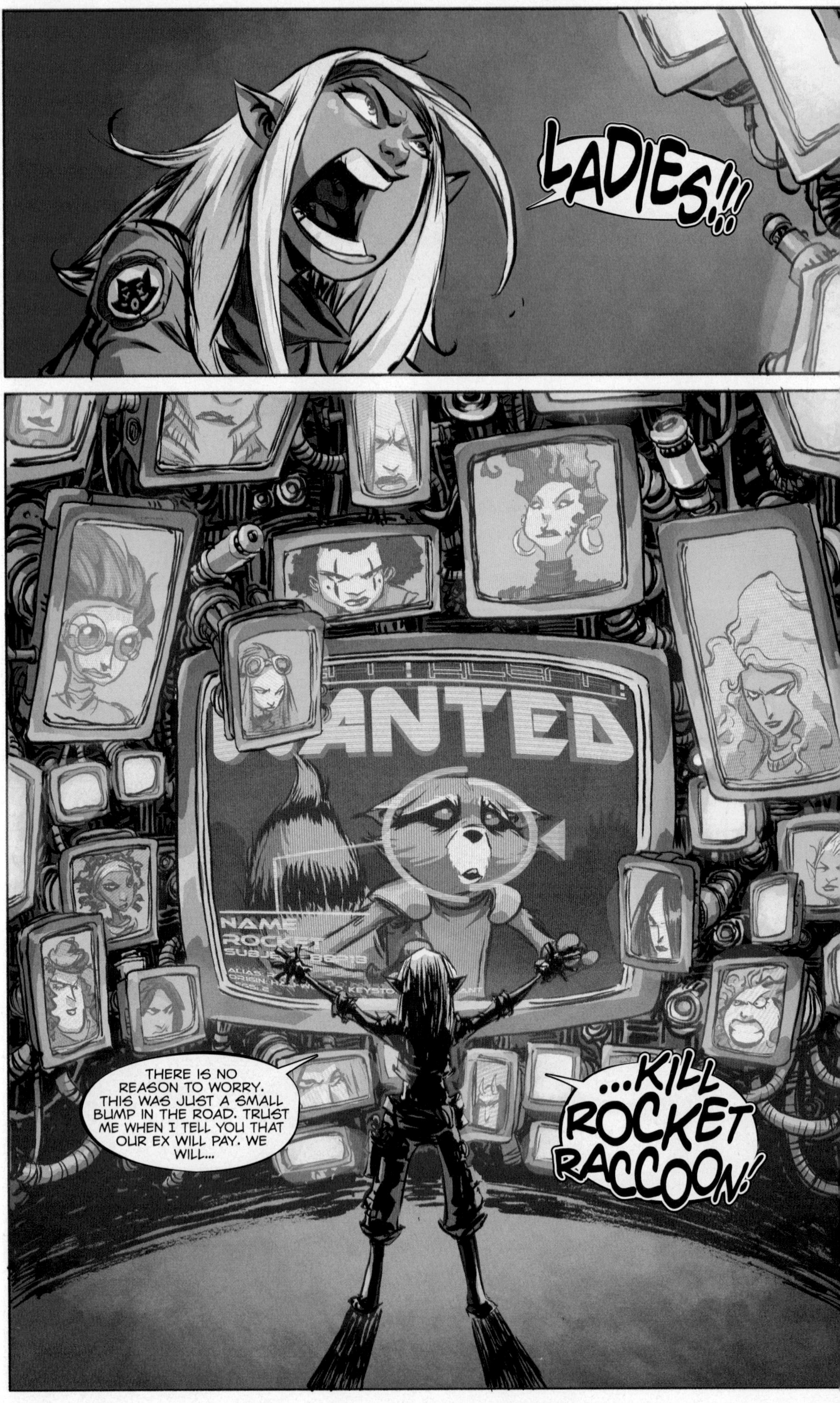
LADIES!!!
NAME
ROCKET
THERE IS NO REASON TO WORRY. THIS WAS JUST A SMALL BUMP IN THE ROAD. TRUST ME WHEN I TELL YOU THAT OUR EX WILL PAY. WE WILL...
...KILL ROCKET RACCOON!

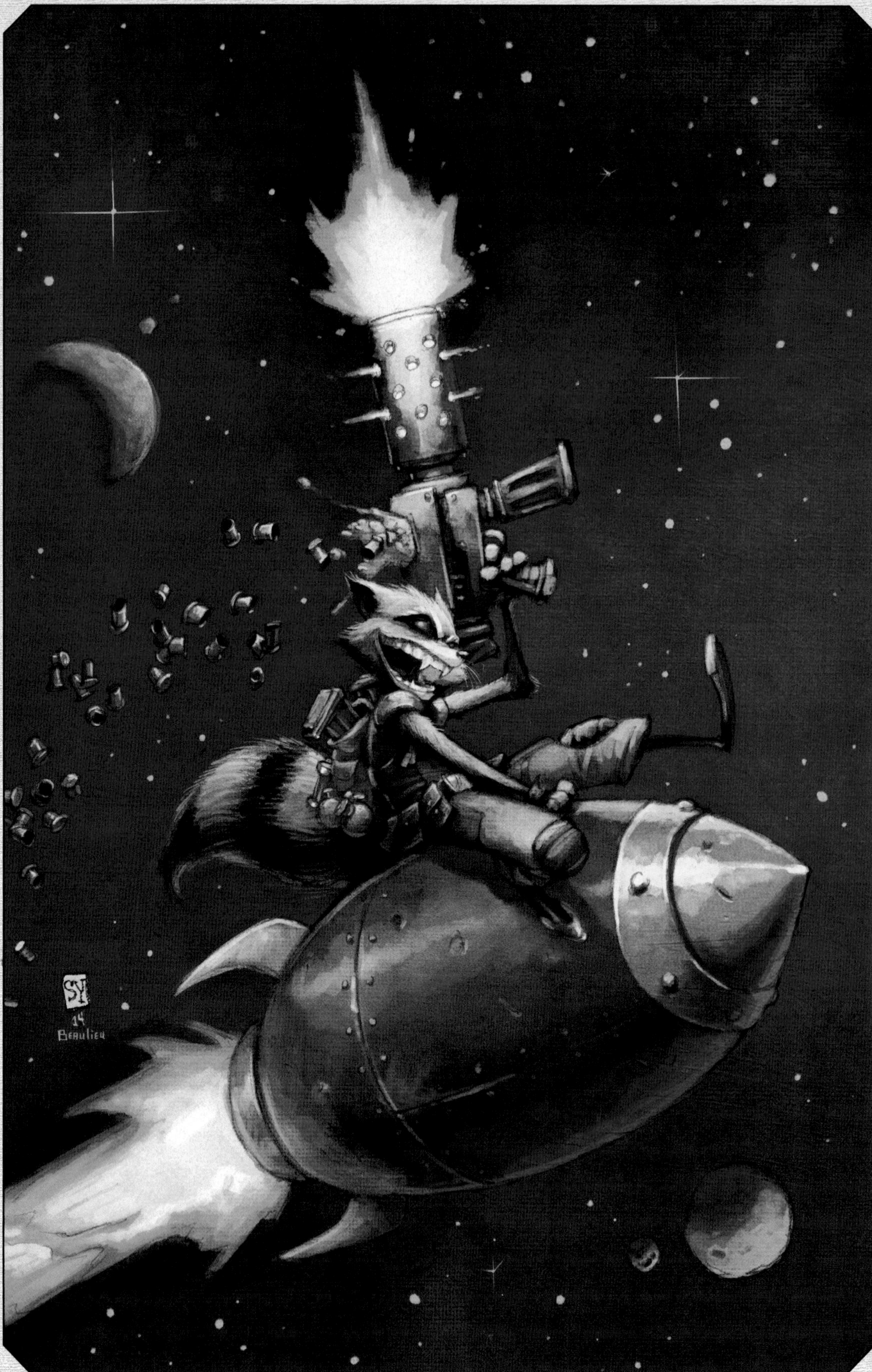
SY
14
BEAULIEU

2

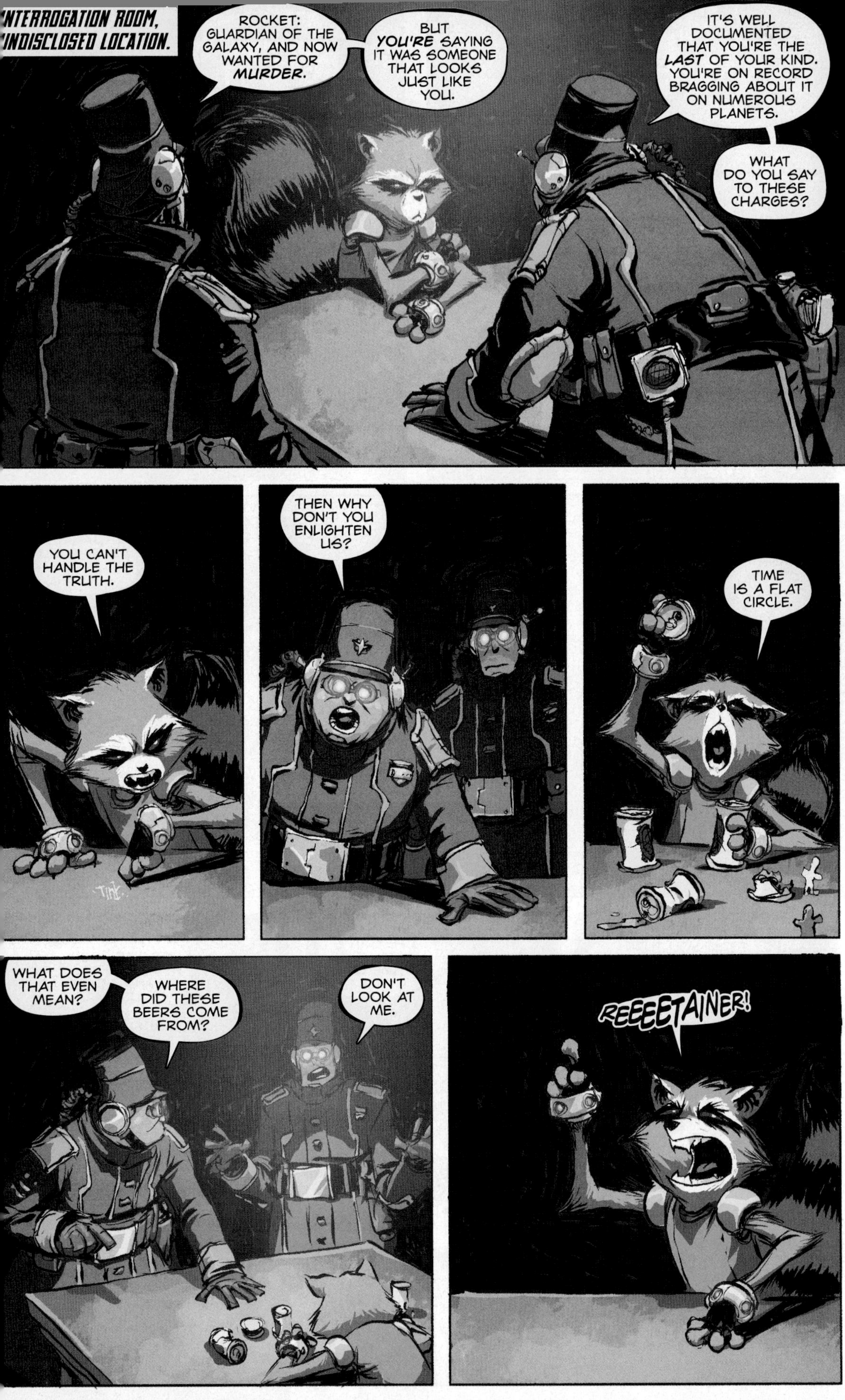
INTERROGATION ROOM, UNDISCLOSED LOCATION.
ROCKET: GUARDIAN OF THE GALAXY, AND NOW WANTED FOR MURDER.
BUT YOU'RE SAYING IT WAS SOMEONE THAT LOOKS JUST LIKE YOU.
IT'S WELL DOCUMENTED THAT YOU'RE THE LAST OF YOUR KIND. YOU'RE ON RECORD BRAGGING ABOUT IT ON NUMEROUS PLANETS.
WHAT DO YOU SAY TO THESE CHARGES?
YOU CAN'T HANDLE THE TRUTH.
THEN WHY DON'T YOU ENLIGHTEN US?
TIME IS A FLAT CIRCLE.
WHAT DOES THAT EVEN MEAN?
WHERE DID THESE BEERS COME FROM?
DON'T LOOK AT ME.
REEEEETAINER!

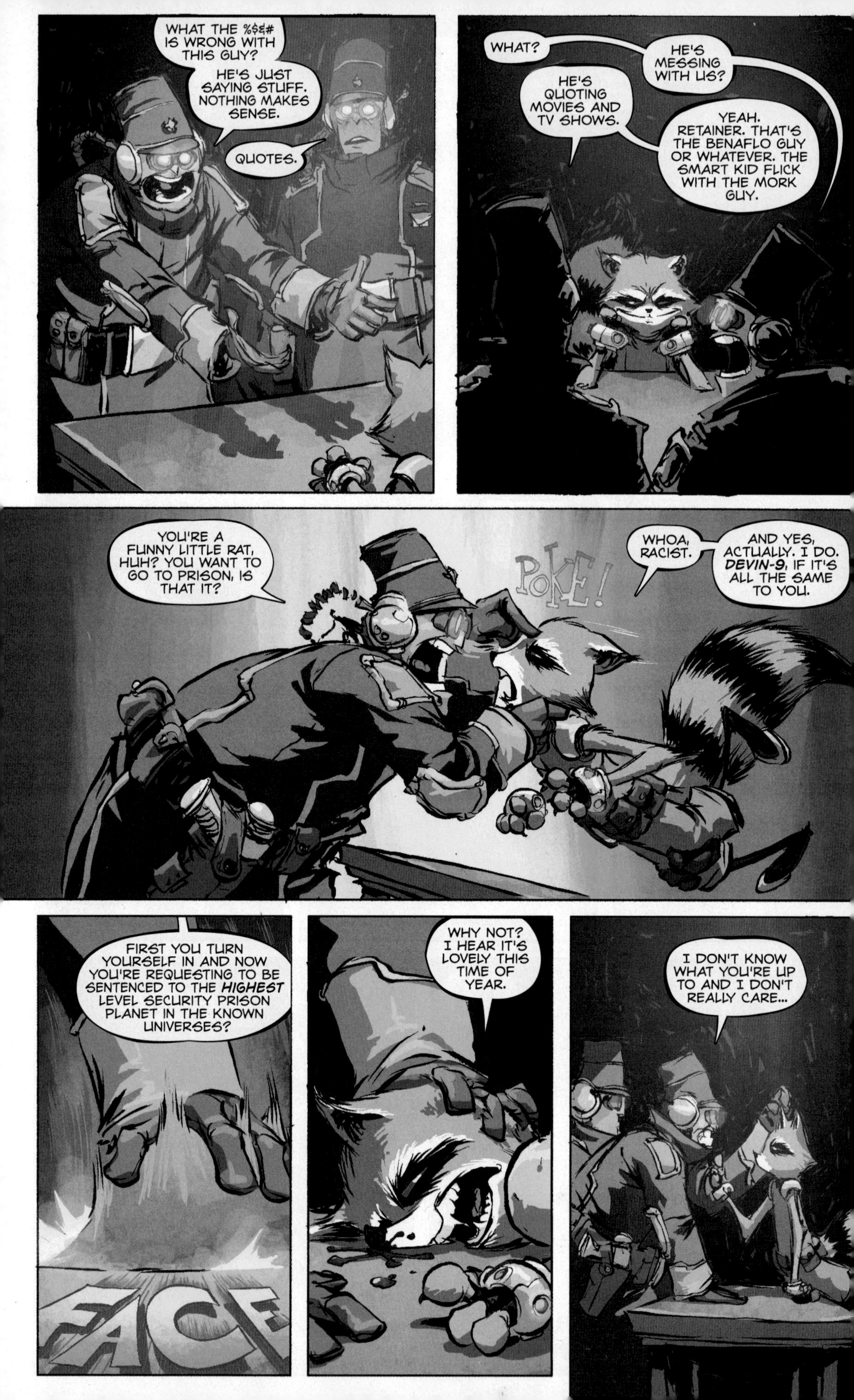
WHAT THE %$&# IS WRONG WITH THIS GUY?
HE'S JUST SAYING STUFF. NOTHING MAKES SENSE.
QUOTES.
WHAT?
HE'S QUOTING MOVIES AND TV SHOWS.
HE'S MESSING WITH US?
YEAH. RETAINER. THAT'S THE BENAFLO GUY OR WHATEVER. THE SMART KID FLICK WITH THE MORK GUY.
YOU'RE A FUNNY LITTLE RAT, HUH? YOU WANT TO GO TO PRISON, IS THAT IT?
POKE!
WHOA, RACIST.
AND YES, ACTUALLY. I DO. DEVIN-9, IF IT'S ALL THE SAME TO YOU.
FIRST YOU TURN YOURSELF IN AND NOW YOU'RE REQUESTING TO BE SENTENCED TO THE HIGHEST LEVEL SECURITY PRISON PLANET IN THE KNOWN UNIVERSES?
FACE
WHY NOT? I HEAR IT'S LOVELY THIS TIME OF YEAR.
I DON'T KNOW WHAT YOU'RE UP TO AND I DON'T REALLY CARE...

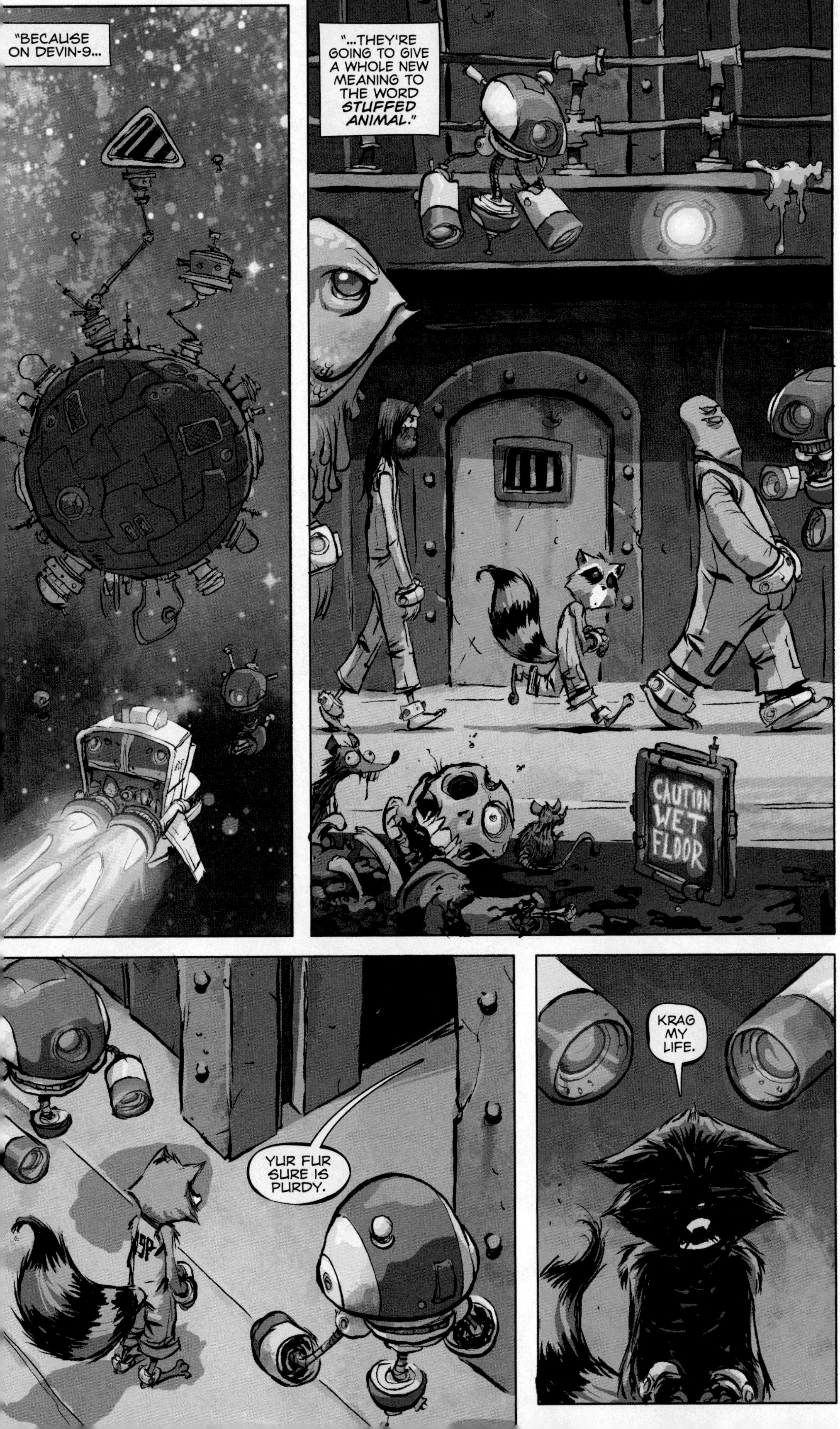
"BECAUSE ON DEVIN-9...
"...THEY'RE GOING TO GIVE A WHOLE NEW MEANING TO THE WORD *STUFFED ANIMAL.*"
CAUTION WET FLOOR
YUR FUR SURE IS PURDY.
KRAG MY LIFE.

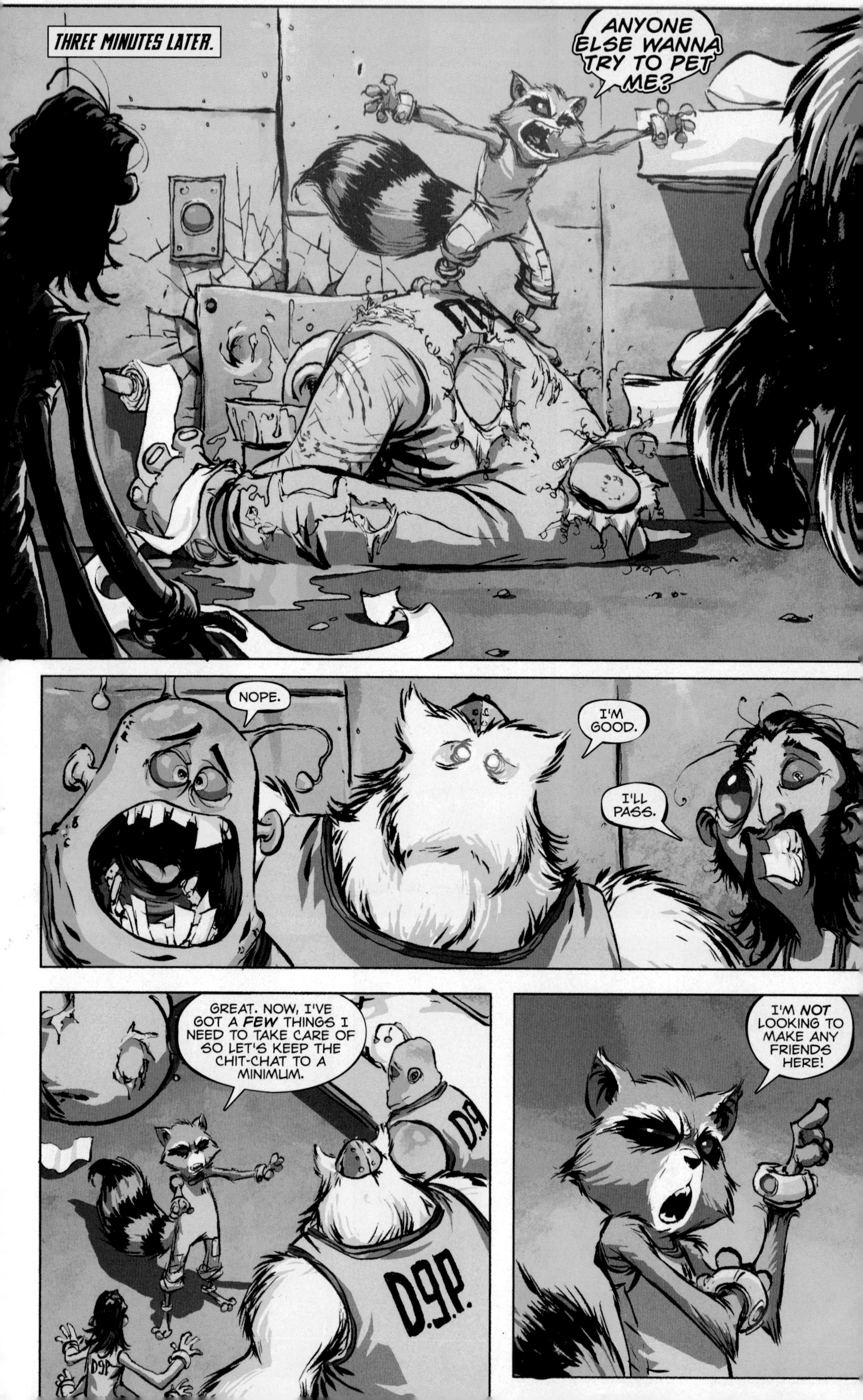
THREE MINUTES LATER.
ANYONE ELSE WANNA TRY TO PET ME?
NOPE.
I'M GOOD.
I'LL PASS.
GREAT. NOW, I'VE GOT A FEW THINGS I NEED TO TAKE CARE OF SO LET'S KEEP THE CHIT-CHAT TO A MINIMUM.
D.9.P.
I'M NOT LOOKING TO MAKE ANY FRIENDS HERE!

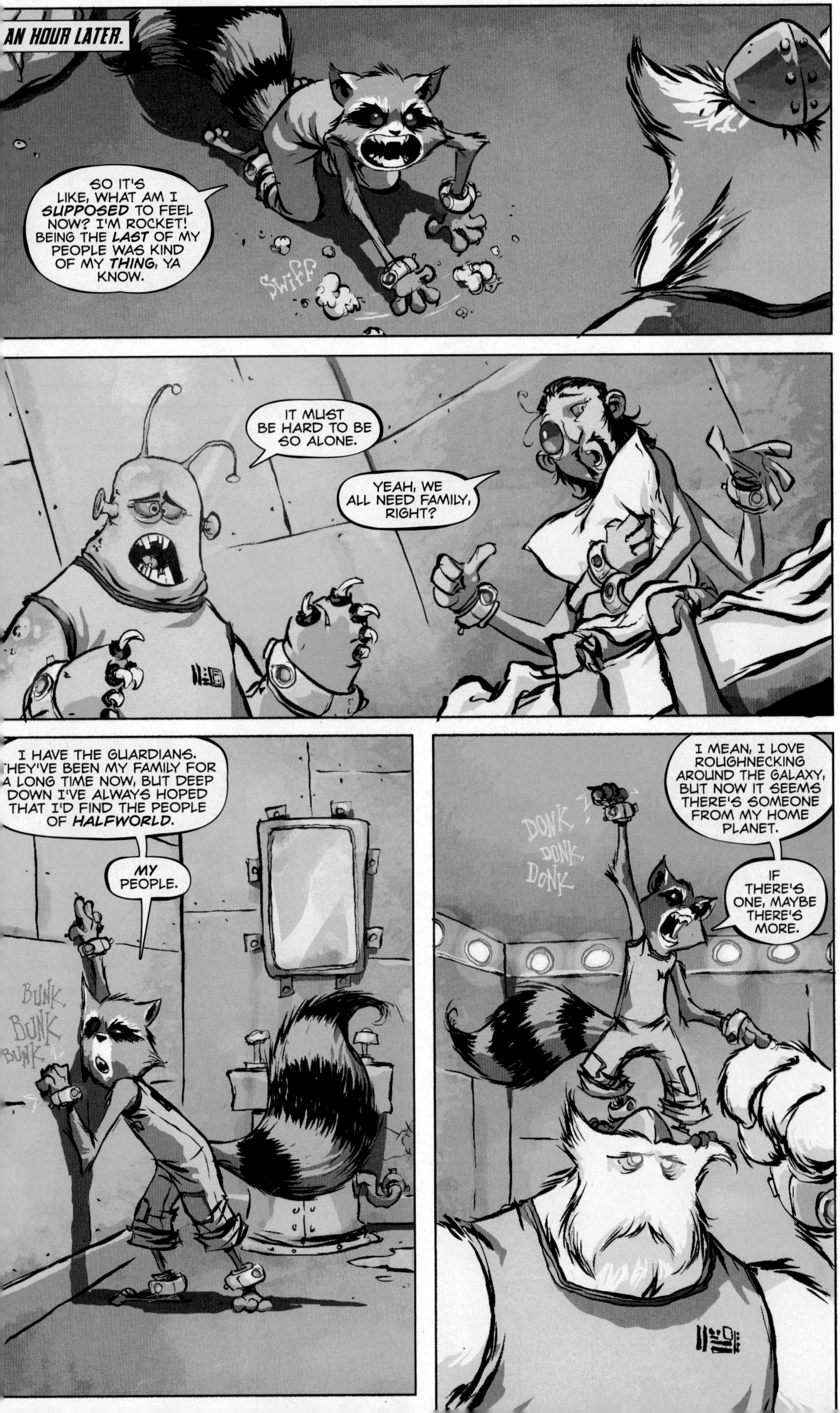
AN HOUR LATER.
SO IT'S LIKE, WHAT AM I SUPPOSED TO FEEL NOW? I'M ROCKET! BEING THE LAST OF MY PEOPLE WAS KIND OF MY THING, YA KNOW.
SWIFF
IT MUST BE HARD TO BE SO ALONE.
YEAH, WE ALL NEED FAMILY, RIGHT?
I HAVE THE GUARDIANS. THEY'VE BEEN MY FAMILY FOR A LONG TIME NOW, BUT DEEP DOWN I'VE ALWAYS HOPED THAT I'D FIND THE PEOPLE OF HALFWORLD.
MY PEOPLE.
BUNK BUNK BUNK
I MEAN, I LOVE ROUGHNECKING AROUND THE GALAXY, BUT NOW IT SEEMS THERE'S SOMEONE FROM MY HOME PLANET.
DONK DONK DONK
IF THERE'S ONE, MAYBE THERE'S MORE.

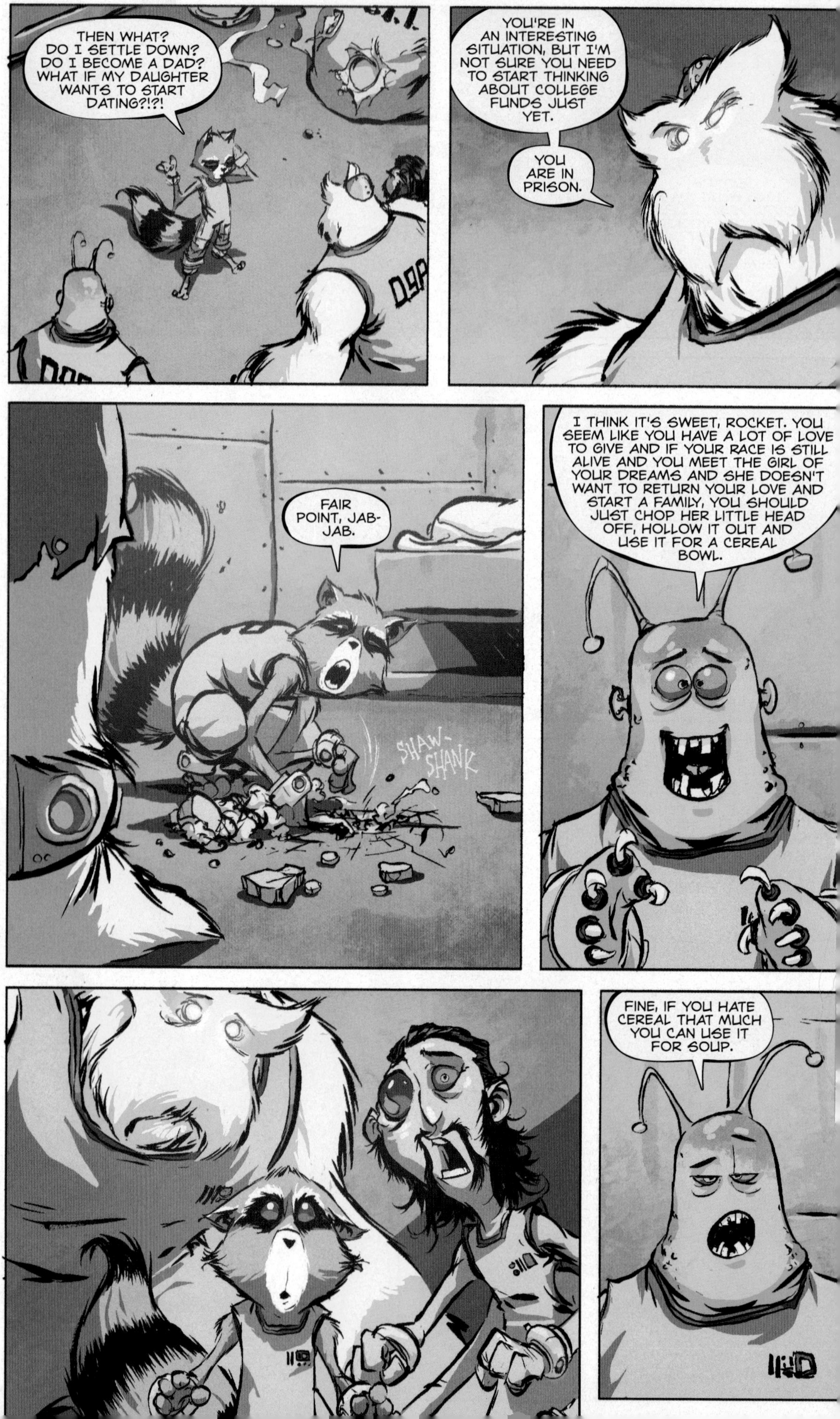
THEN WHAT? DO I SETTLE DOWN? DO I BECOME A DAD? WHAT IF MY DAUGHTER WANTS TO START DATING?!?!
YOU'RE IN AN INTERESTING SITUATION, BUT I'M NOT SURE YOU NEED TO START THINKING ABOUT COLLEGE FUNDS JUST YET.
YOU ARE IN PRISON.
FAIR POINT, JAB-JAB.
SHAW-SHANK
I THINK IT'S SWEET, ROCKET. YOU SEEM LIKE YOU HAVE A LOT OF LOVE TO GIVE AND IF YOUR RACE IS STILL ALIVE AND YOU MEET THE GIRL OF YOUR DREAMS AND SHE DOESN'T WANT TO RETURN YOUR LOVE AND START A FAMILY, YOU SHOULD JUST CHOP HER LITTLE HEAD OFF, HOLLOW IT OUT AND USE IT FOR A CEREAL BOWL.
FINE, IF YOU HATE CEREAL THAT MUCH YOU CAN USE IT FOR SOUP.

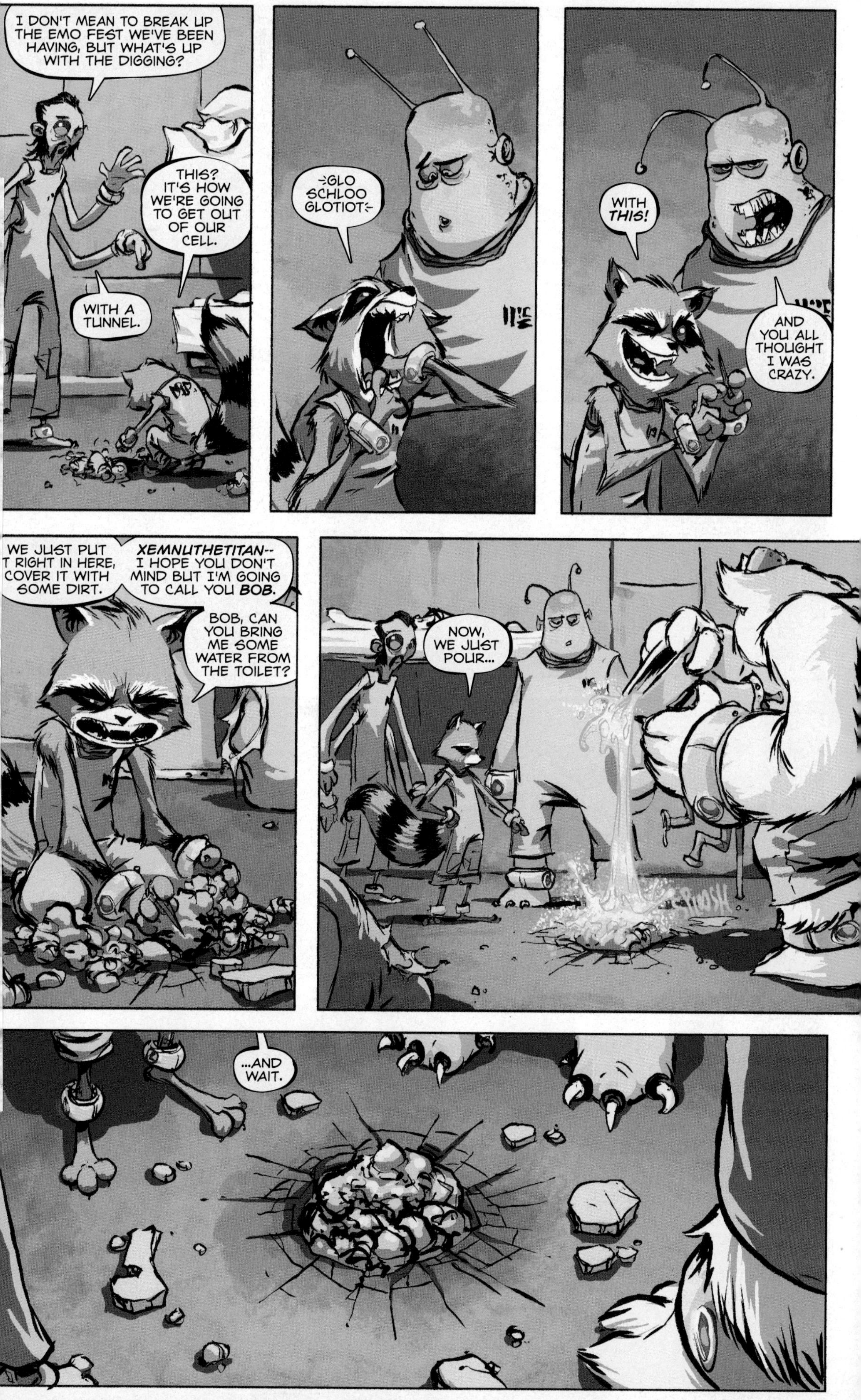

I DON'T MEAN TO BREAK UP THE EMO FEST WE'VE BEEN HAVING, BUT WHAT'S UP WITH THE DIGGING?
THIS? IT'S HOW WE'RE GOING TO GET OUT OF OUR CELL.
WITH A TUNNEL.
GLO SCHLOO GLOTIOT
WITH THIS!
AND YOU ALL THOUGHT I WAS CRAZY.
WE JUST PUT IT RIGHT IN HERE, COVER IT WITH SOME DIRT.
XEMNUTHETITAN-- I HOPE YOU DON'T MIND BUT I'M GOING TO CALL YOU BOB.
BOB, CAN YOU BRING ME SOME WATER FROM THE TOILET?
NOW, WE JUST POUR...
SPLOOSH
...AND WAIT.

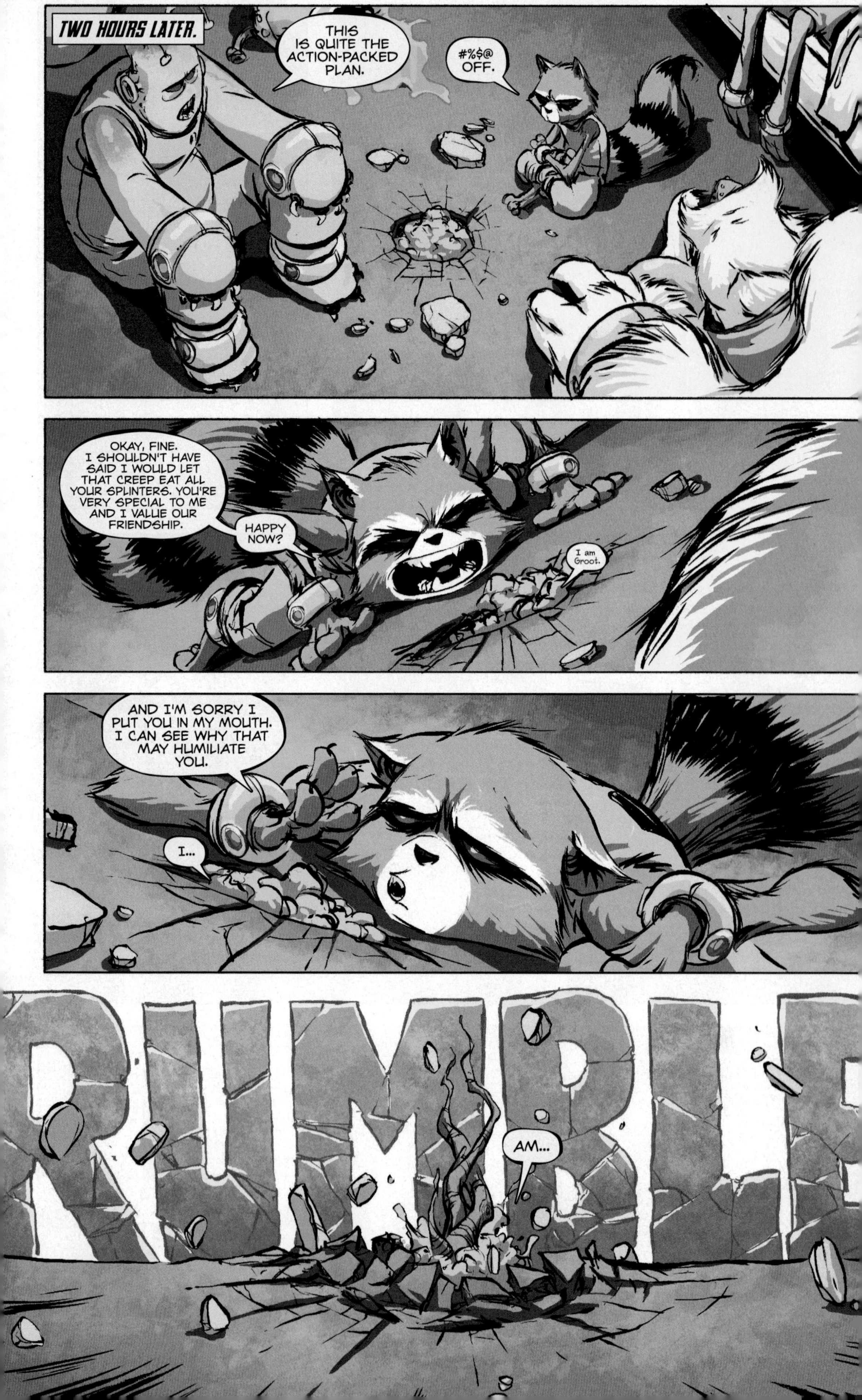
TWO HOURS LATER.
THIS IS QUITE THE ACTION-PACKED PLAN.
#%$@ OFF.
OKAY, FINE. I SHOULDN'T HAVE SAID I WOULD LET THAT CREEP EAT ALL YOUR SPLINTERS. YOU'RE VERY SPECIAL TO ME AND I VALUE OUR FRIENDSHIP.
HAPPY NOW?
I am Groot.
AND I'M SORRY I PUT YOU IN MY MOUTH. I CAN SEE WHY THAT MAY HUMILIATE YOU.
I...
RUMBLE
AM...

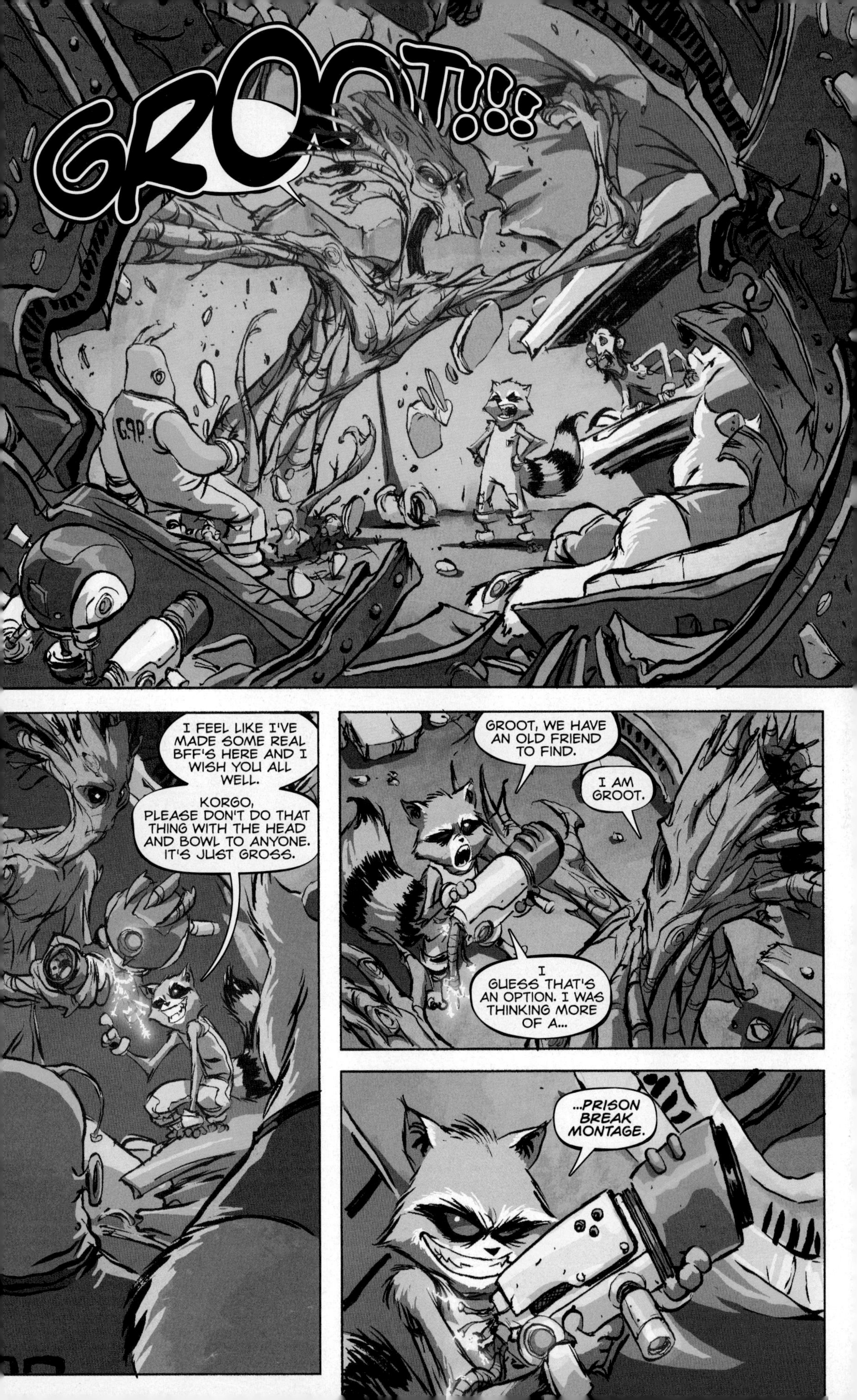
GROOOT!!!
I FEEL LIKE I'VE MADE SOME REAL BFF'S HERE AND I WISH YOU ALL WELL.
KORGO, PLEASE DON'T DO THAT THING WITH THE HEAD AND BOWL TO ANYONE. IT'S JUST GROSS.
GROOT, WE HAVE AN OLD FRIEND TO FIND.
I AM GROOT.
I GUESS THAT'S AN OPTION. I WAS THINKING MORE OF A...
...PRISON BREAK MONTAGE.

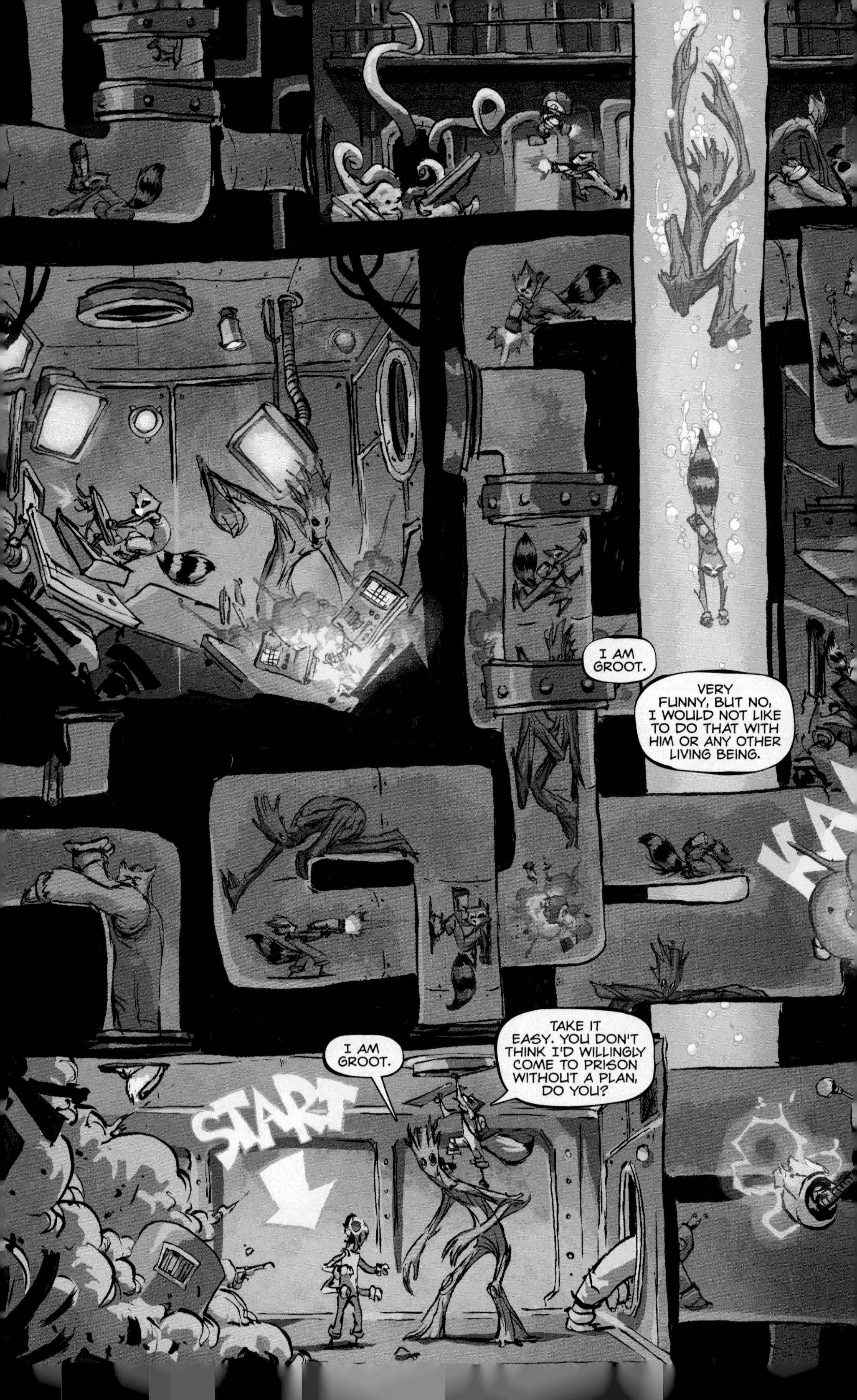
I AM GROOT.
VERY FUNNY, BUT NO, I WOULD NOT LIKE TO DO THAT WITH HIM OR ANY OTHER LIVING BEING.
START
I AM GROOT.
TAKE IT EASY. YOU DON'T THINK I'D WILLINGLY COME TO PRISON WITHOUT A PLAN, DO YOU?

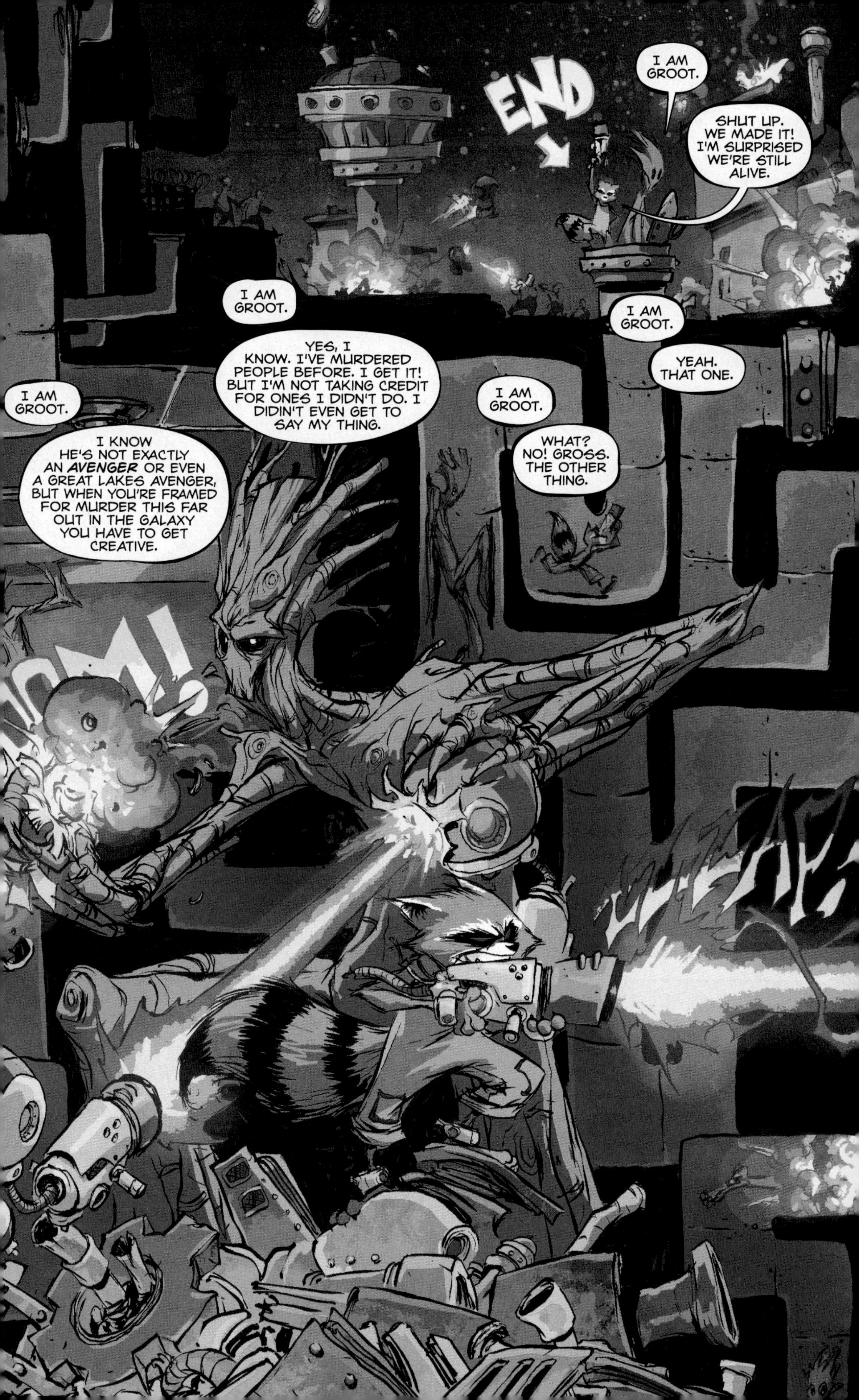
END
I AM GROOT.
SHUT UP. WE MADE IT! I'M SURPRISED WE'RE STILL ALIVE.
I AM GROOT.
I KNOW HE'S NOT EXACTLY AN AVENGER OR EVEN A GREAT LAKES AVENGER, BUT WHEN YOU'RE FRAMED FOR MURDER THIS FAR OUT IN THE GALAXY YOU HAVE TO GET CREATIVE.
I AM GROOT.
YES, I KNOW. I'VE MURDERED PEOPLE BEFORE. I GET IT! BUT I'M NOT TAKING CREDIT FOR ONES I DIDN'T DO. I DIDIN'T EVEN GET TO SAY MY THING.
I AM GROOT.
WHAT? NO! GROSS. THE OTHER THING.
I AM GROOT.
YEAH. THAT ONE.

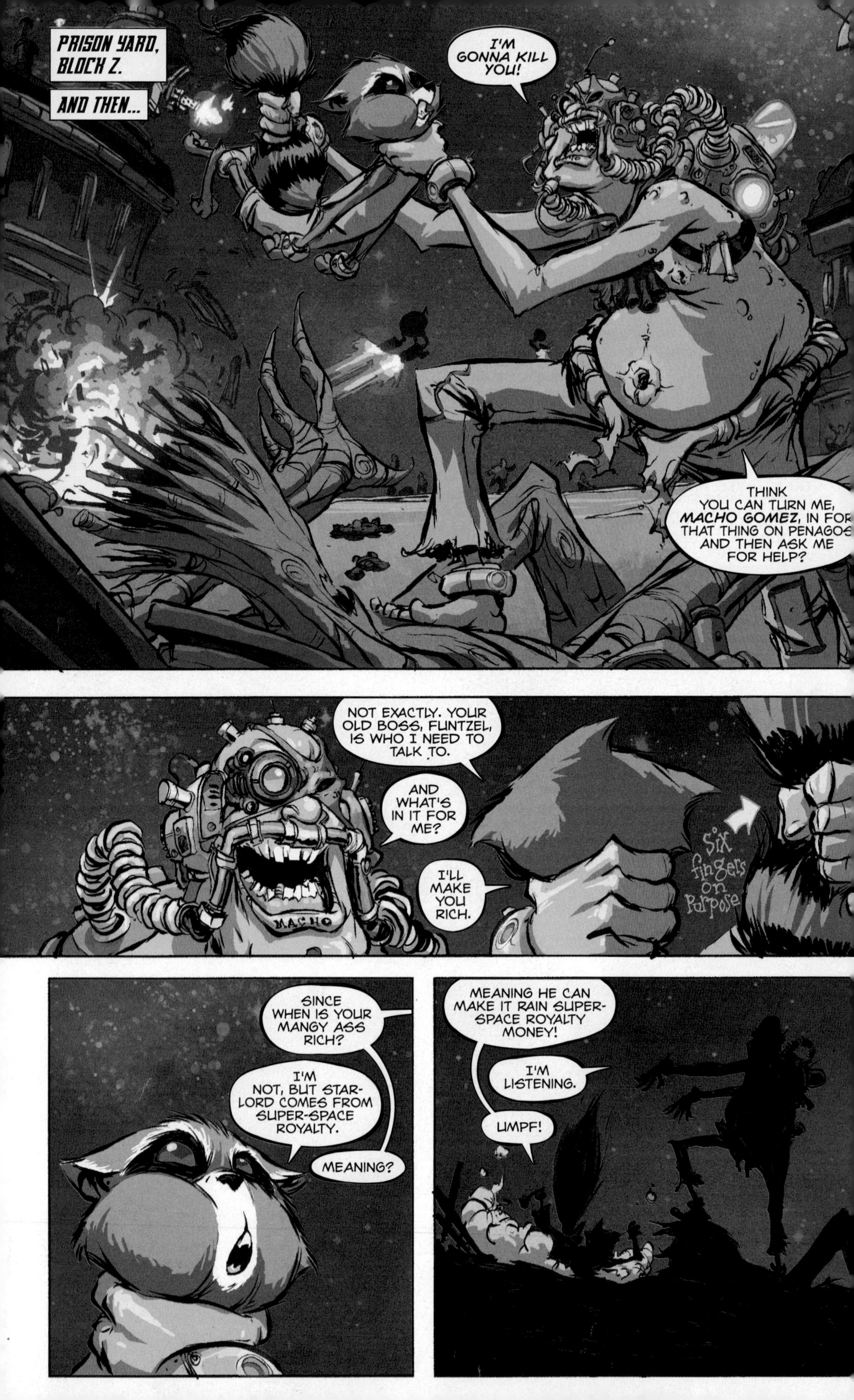
PRISON YARD, BLOCK Z.
AND THEN...
I'M GONNA KILL YOU!
THINK YOU CAN TURN ME, MACHO GOMEZ, IN FOR THAT THING ON PENAGOS AND THEN ASK ME FOR HELP?
NOT EXACTLY. YOUR OLD BOSS, FUNTZEL, IS WHO I NEED TO TALK TO.
AND WHAT'S IN IT FOR ME?
I'LL MAKE YOU RICH.
MACHO
Six fingers on Purpose
SINCE WHEN IS YOUR MANGY ASS RICH?
I'M NOT, BUT STAR-LORD COMES FROM SUPER-SPACE ROYALTY.
MEANING?
MEANING HE CAN MAKE IT RAIN SUPER-SPACE ROYALTY MONEY!
I'M LISTENING.
UMPF!

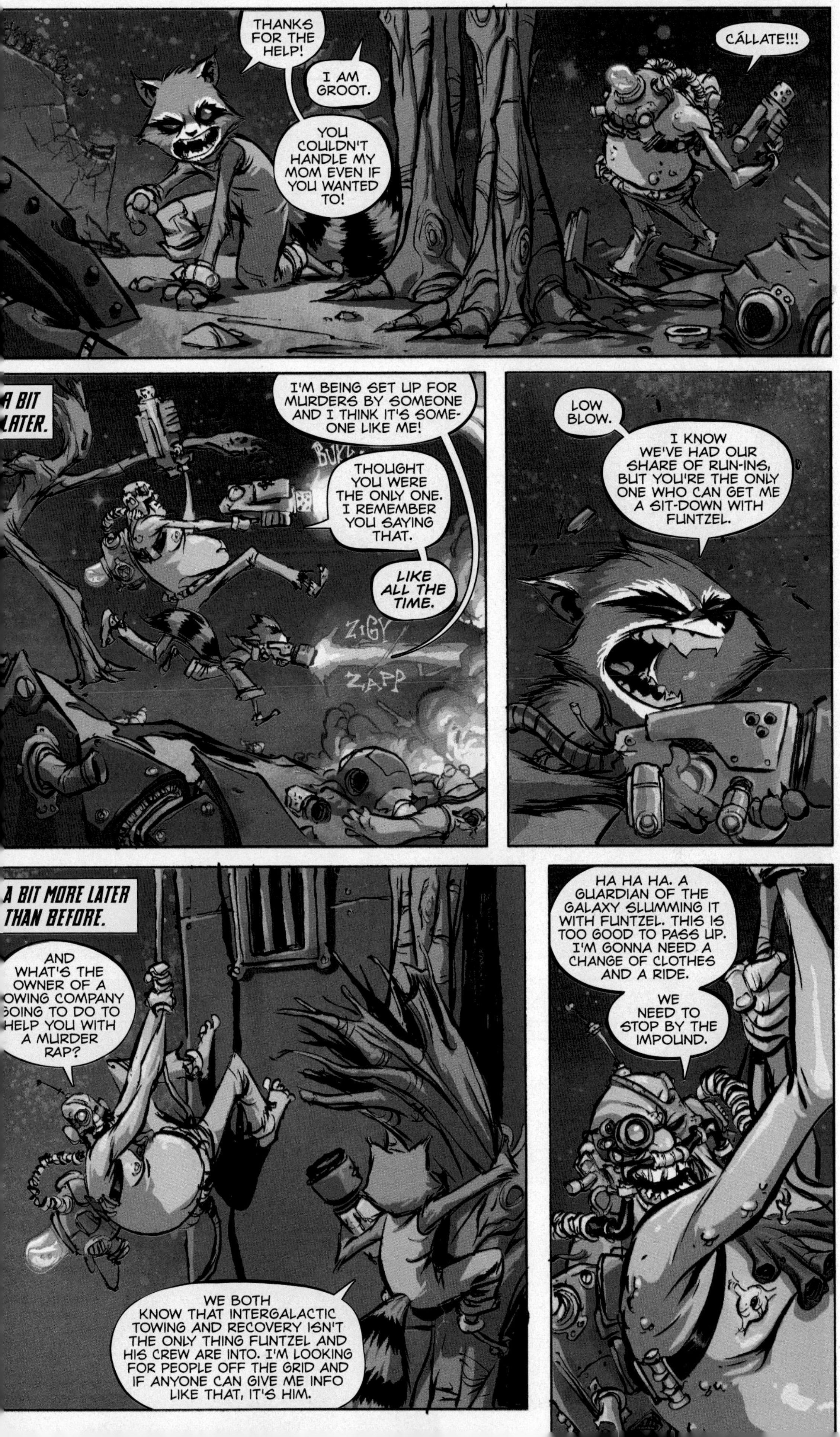
THANKS FOR THE HELP!
I AM GROOT.
YOU COULDN'T HANDLE MY MOM EVEN IF YOU WANTED TO!
CÁLLATE!!!
A BIT LATER.
I'M BEING SET UP FOR MURDERS BY SOMEONE AND I THINK IT'S SOME-ONE LIKE ME!
THOUGHT YOU WERE THE ONLY ONE. I REMEMBER YOU SAYING THAT.
LIKE ALL THE TIME.
ZIGY
ZAPP
LOW BLOW.
I KNOW WE'VE HAD OUR SHARE OF RUN-INS, BUT YOU'RE THE ONLY ONE WHO CAN GET ME A SIT-DOWN WITH FUNTZEL.
A BIT MORE LATER THAN BEFORE.
AND WHAT'S THE OWNER OF A TOWING COMPANY GOING TO DO TO HELP YOU WITH A MURDER RAP?
WE BOTH KNOW THAT INTERGALACTIC TOWING AND RECOVERY ISN'T THE ONLY THING FUNTZEL AND HIS CREW ARE INTO. I'M LOOKING FOR PEOPLE OFF THE GRID AND IF ANYONE CAN GIVE ME INFO LIKE THAT, IT'S HIM.
HA HA HA. A GUARDIAN OF THE GALAXY SLUMMING IT WITH FUNTZEL. THIS IS TOO GOOD TO PASS UP. I'M GONNA NEED A CHANGE OF CLOTHES AND A RIDE.
WE NEED TO STOP BY THE IMPOUND.

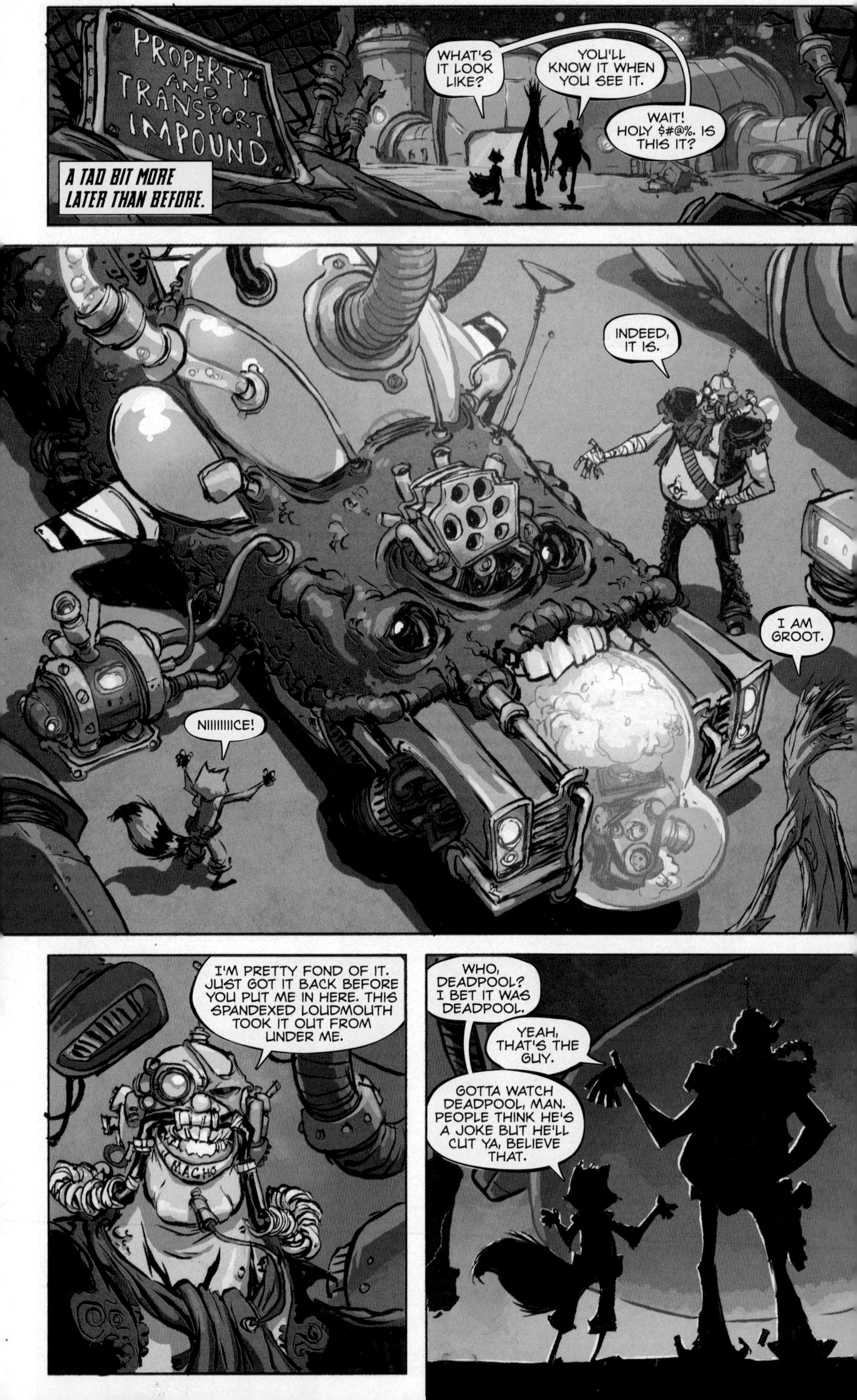
PROPERTY AND TRANSPORT IMPOUND
A TAD BIT MORE LATER THAN BEFORE.
WHAT'S IT LOOK LIKE?
YOU'LL KNOW IT WHEN YOU SEE IT.
WAIT! HOLY $#@%. IS THIS IT?
INDEED, IT IS.
I AM GROOT.
NIIIIIIICE!
I'M PRETTY FOND OF IT. JUST GOT IT BACK BEFORE YOU PUT ME IN HERE. THIS SPANDEXED LOUDMOUTH TOOK IT OUT FROM UNDER ME.
MACHO
WHO, DEADPOOL? I BET IT WAS DEADPOOL.
YEAH, THAT'S THE GUY.
GOTTA WATCH DEADPOOL, MAN. PEOPLE THINK HE'S A JOKE BUT HE'LL CUT YA, BELIEVE THAT.

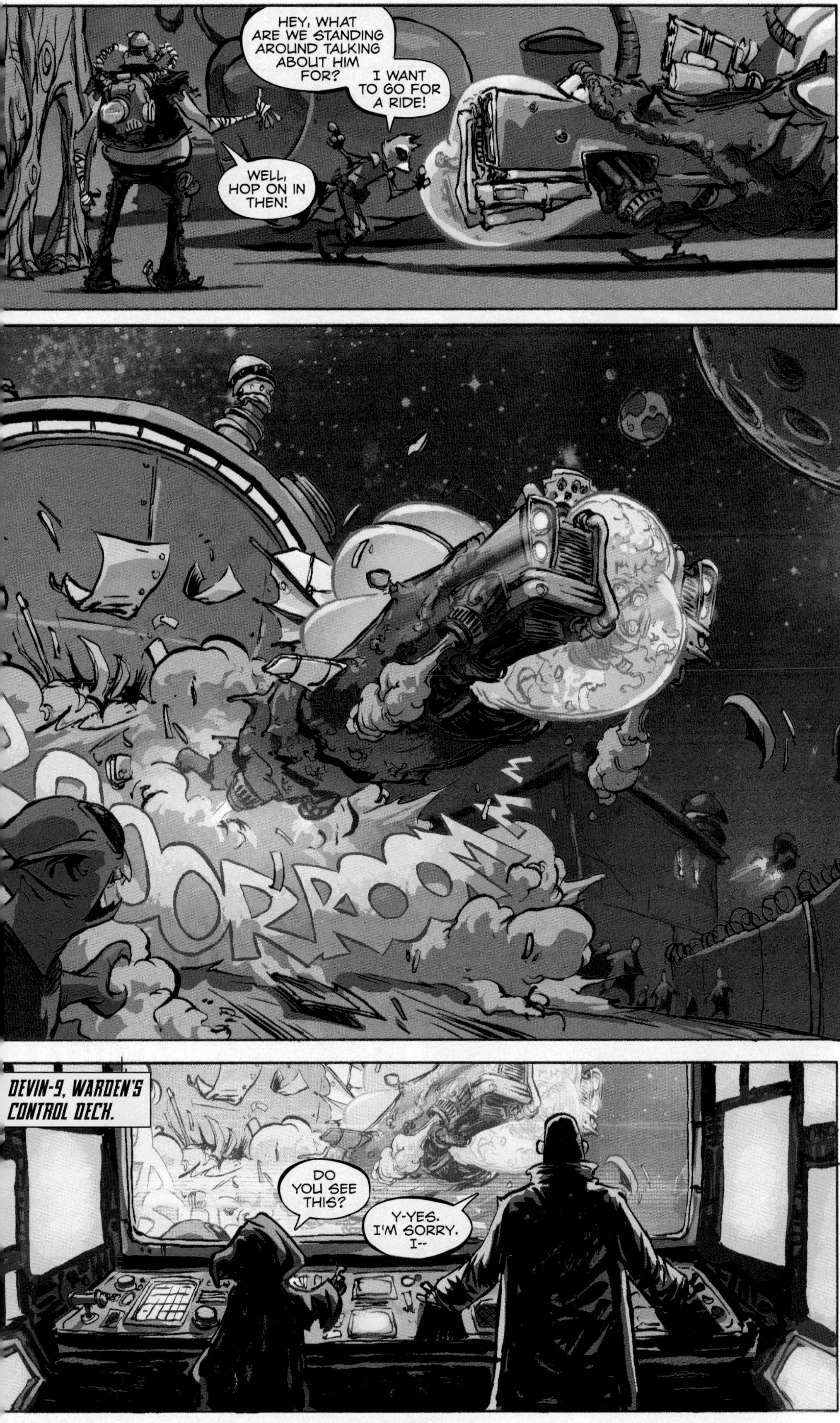
HEY, WHAT ARE WE STANDING AROUND TALKING ABOUT HIM FOR?
I WANT TO GO FOR A RIDE!
WELL, HOP ON IN THEN!
DEVIN-9, WARDEN'S CONTROL DECK.
DO YOU SEE THIS?
Y-YES. I'M SORRY. I--

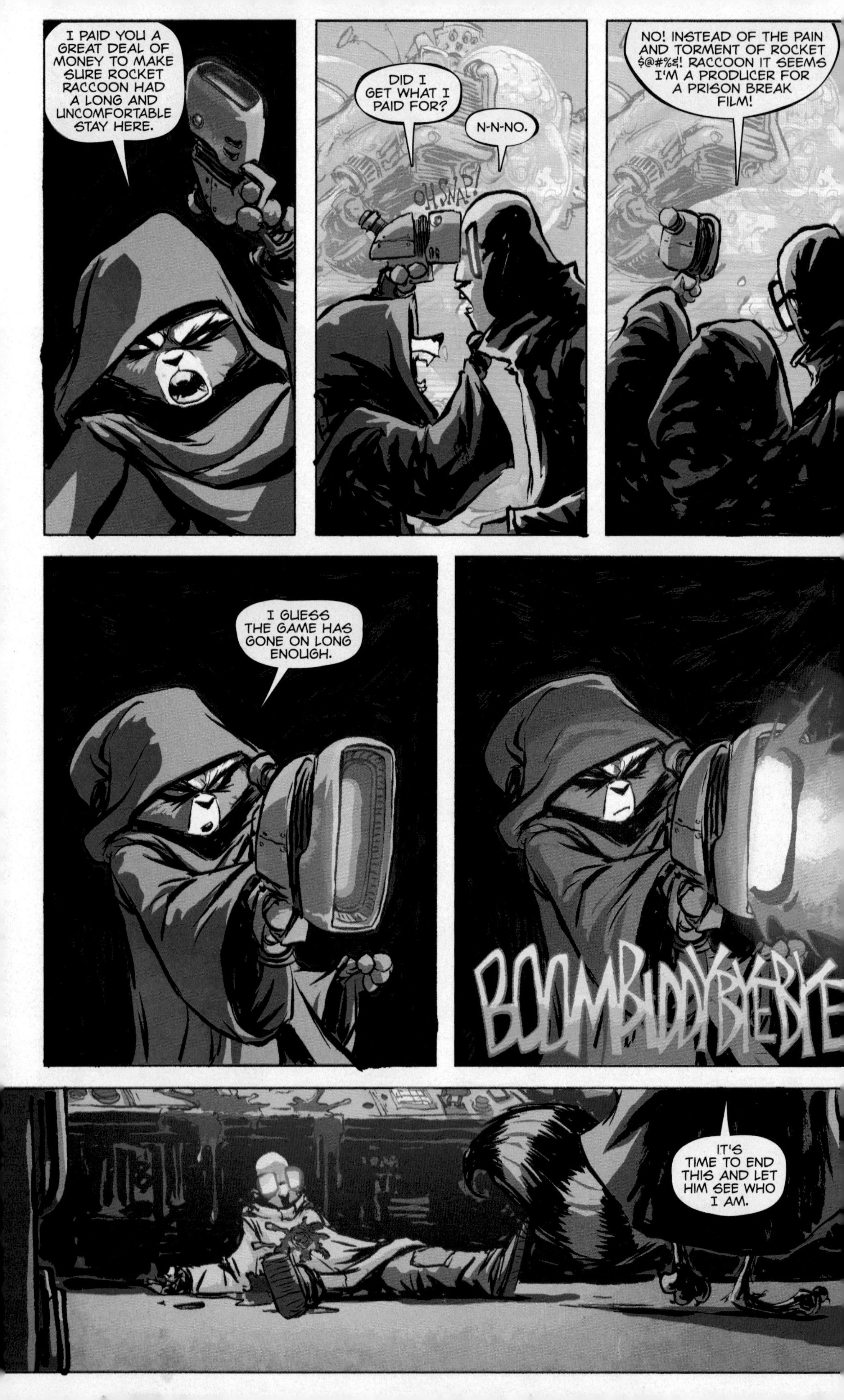
I PAID YOU A GREAT DEAL OF MONEY TO MAKE SURE ROCKET RACCOON HAD A LONG AND UNCOMFORTABLE STAY HERE.
DID I GET WHAT I PAID FOR?
N-N-NO.
OH SNAP!
NO! INSTEAD OF THE PAIN AND TORMENT OF ROCKET $@#%&! RACCOON IT SEEMS I'M A PRODUCER FOR A PRISON BREAK FILM!
I GUESS THE GAME HAS GONE ON LONG ENOUGH.
BOOMBIDDYBYEBYE
IT'S TIME TO END THIS AND LET HIM SEE WHO I AM.

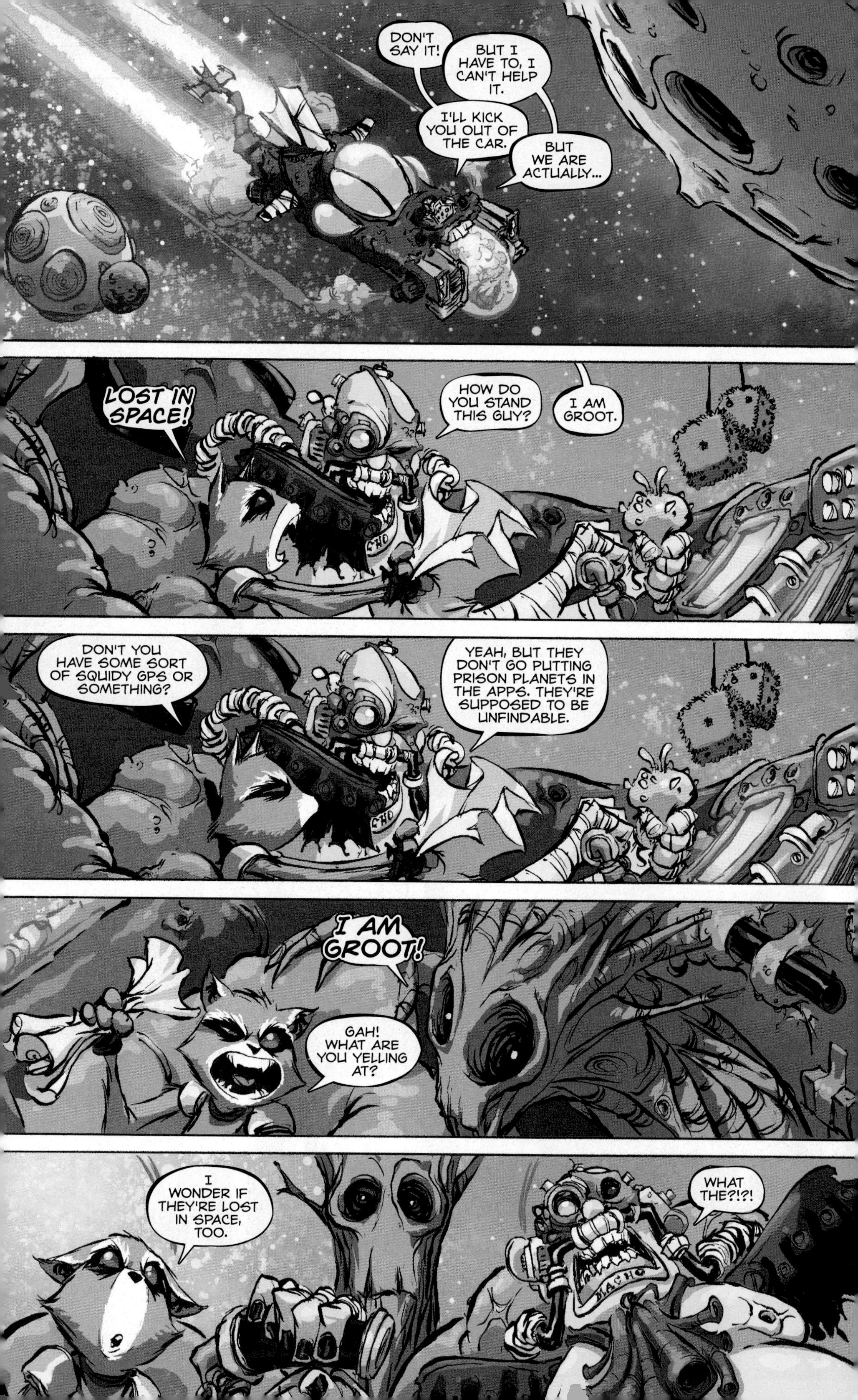
DON'T SAY IT!
BUT I HAVE TO, I CAN'T HELP IT.
I'LL KICK YOU OUT OF THE CAR.
BUT WE ARE ACTUALLY...
LOST IN SPACE!
HOW DO YOU STAND THIS GUY?
I AM GROOT.
DON'T YOU HAVE SOME SORT OF SQUIDY GPS OR SOMETHING?
YEAH, BUT THEY DON'T GO PUTTING PRISON PLANETS IN THE APPS. THEY'RE SUPPOSED TO BE UNFINDABLE.
I AM GROOT!
GAH! WHAT ARE YOU YELLING AT?
I WONDER IF THEY'RE LOST IN SPACE, TOO.
WHAT THE?!?!

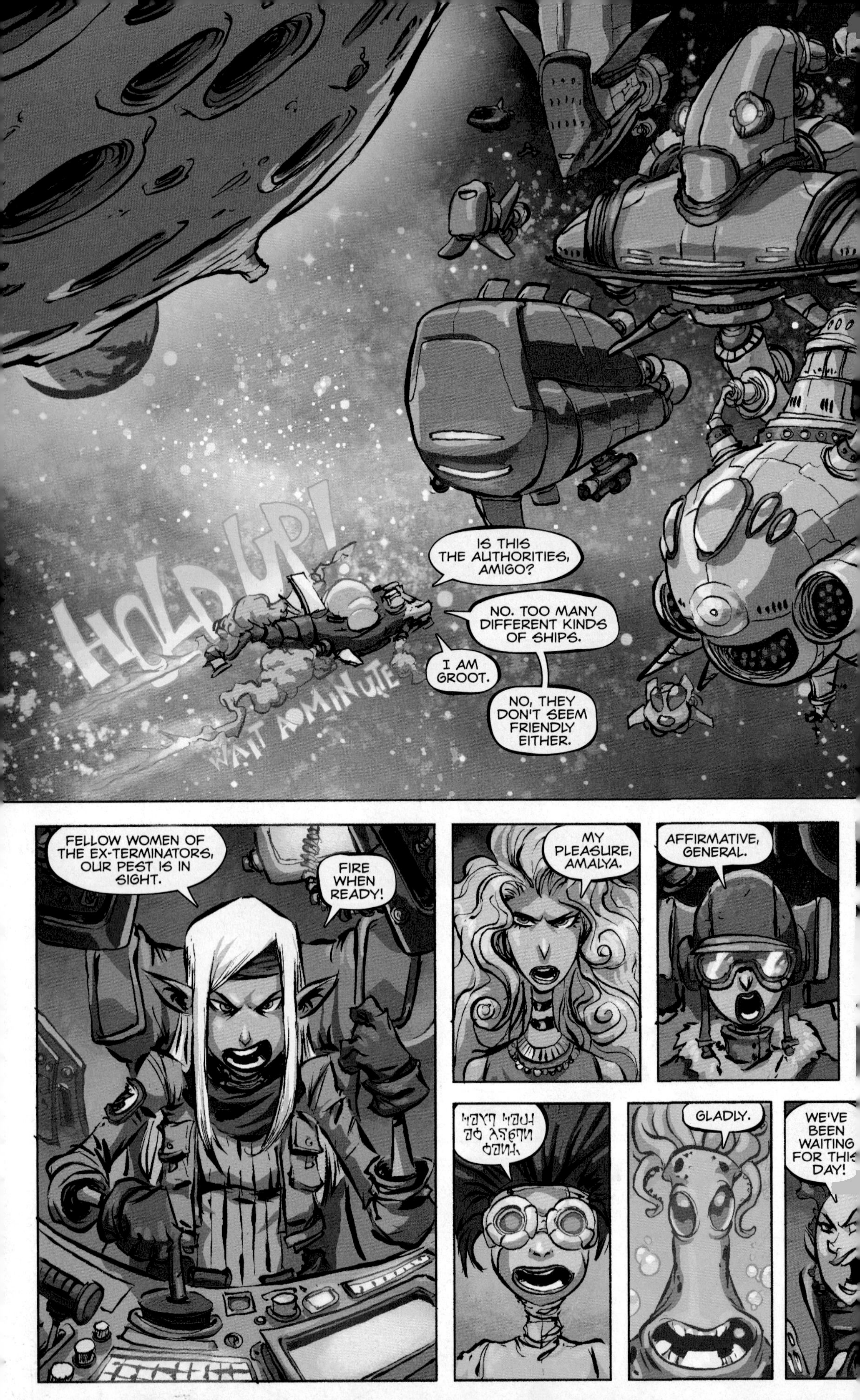
HOLD UP!
WAIT A MINUTE
IS THIS THE AUTHORITIES, AMIGO?
NO. TOO MANY DIFFERENT KINDS OF SHIPS.
I AM GROOT.
NO, THEY DON'T SEEM FRIENDLY EITHER.
FELLOW WOMEN OF THE EX-TERMINATORS, OUR PEST IS IN SIGHT.
FIRE WHEN READY!
MY PLEASURE, AMALYA.
AFFIRMATIVE, GENERAL.
GLADLY.
WE'VE BEEN WAITING FOR THIS DAY!

LET'S BLOW THIS MOTHER !#@%$ UP.

WE'VE BEEN WAITING FOR THIS DAY!

MAY THE DEMONS FEAST ON HIS SOUL THIS DAY.

DONE.

I WILL FIRE, BUT BECAUSE I WANT TO.

NOT BECAUSE YOU ORDERED ME TO. I'M A QUEEN. YOU WERE JUST A PRINCESS WHO RENAMED HERSELF A GENERAL.

THIS IS FOR ME AND MY SISTERS.

LET'S DO THIS.

CHECK.

DONE.

YES, PRINCESS.

AFFIRMATIVE.

WAIT, I THOUGHT THIS WAS A REALITY DATING SHOW. WE'RE NOT HERE TO TRY AND MARRY THE RACCOON?

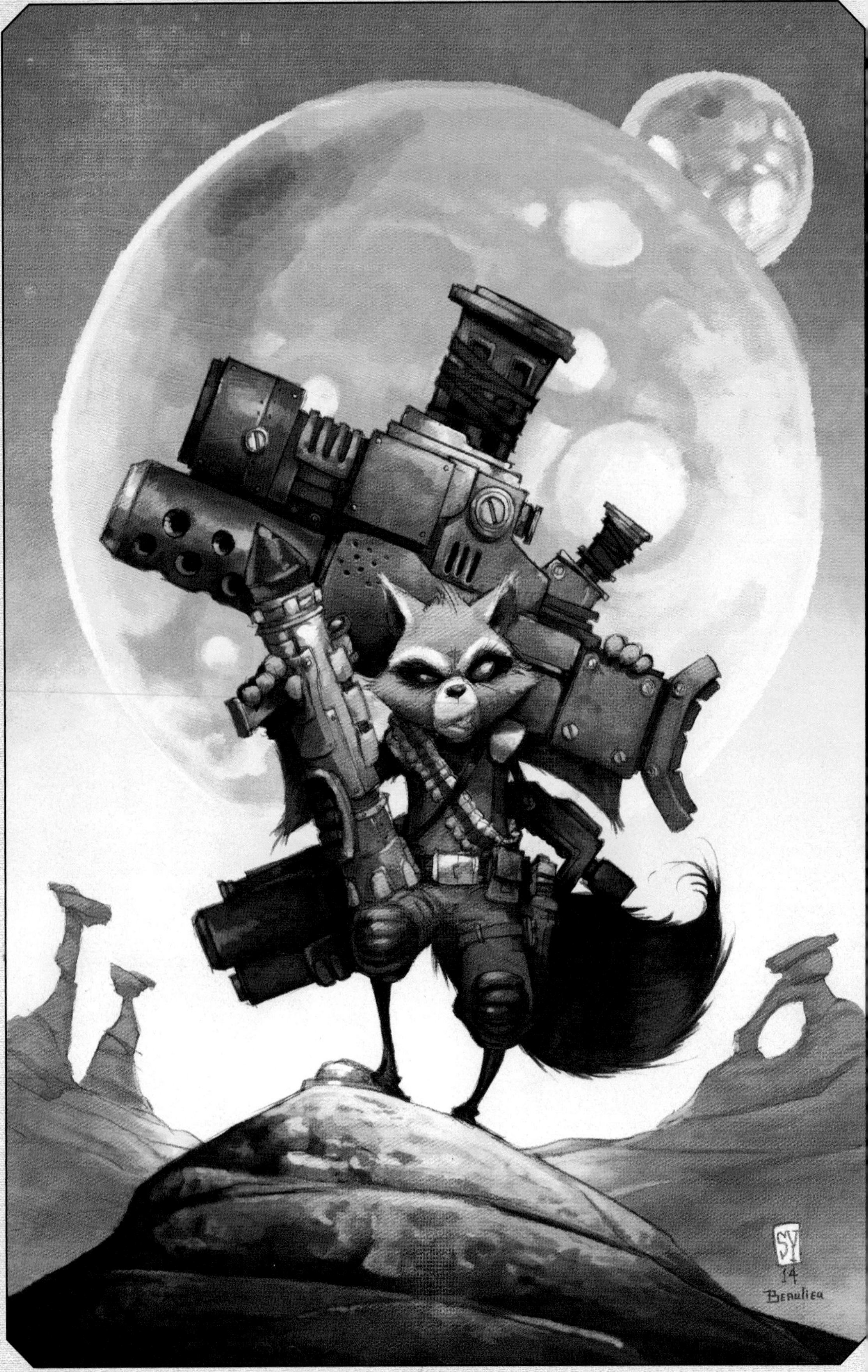
SY
14
Beaulieu

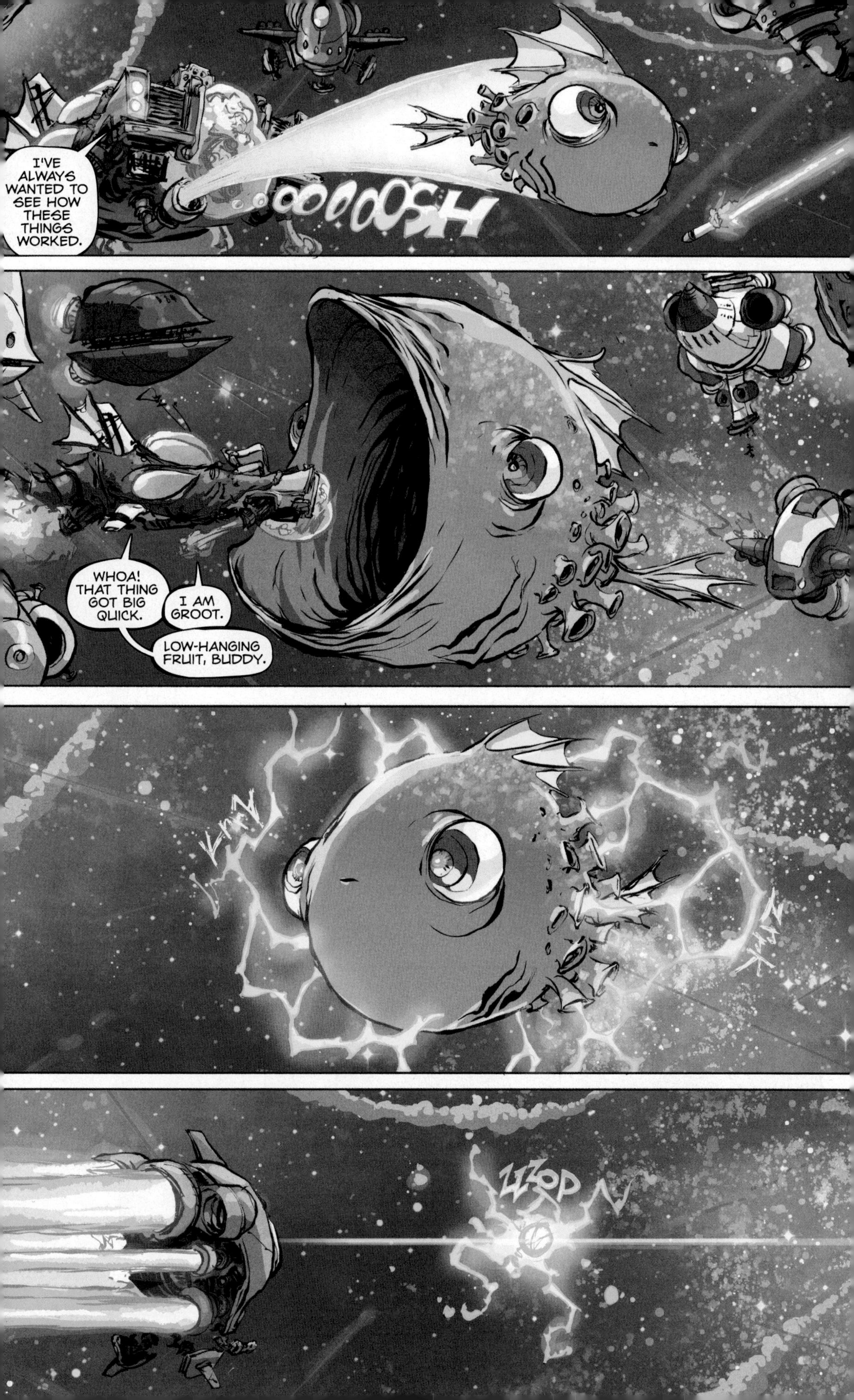

I'VE ALWAYS WANTED TO SEE HOW THESE THINGS WORKED.
WHOA! THAT THING GOT BIG QUICK.
I AM GROOT.
LOW-HANGING FRUIT, BUDDY.

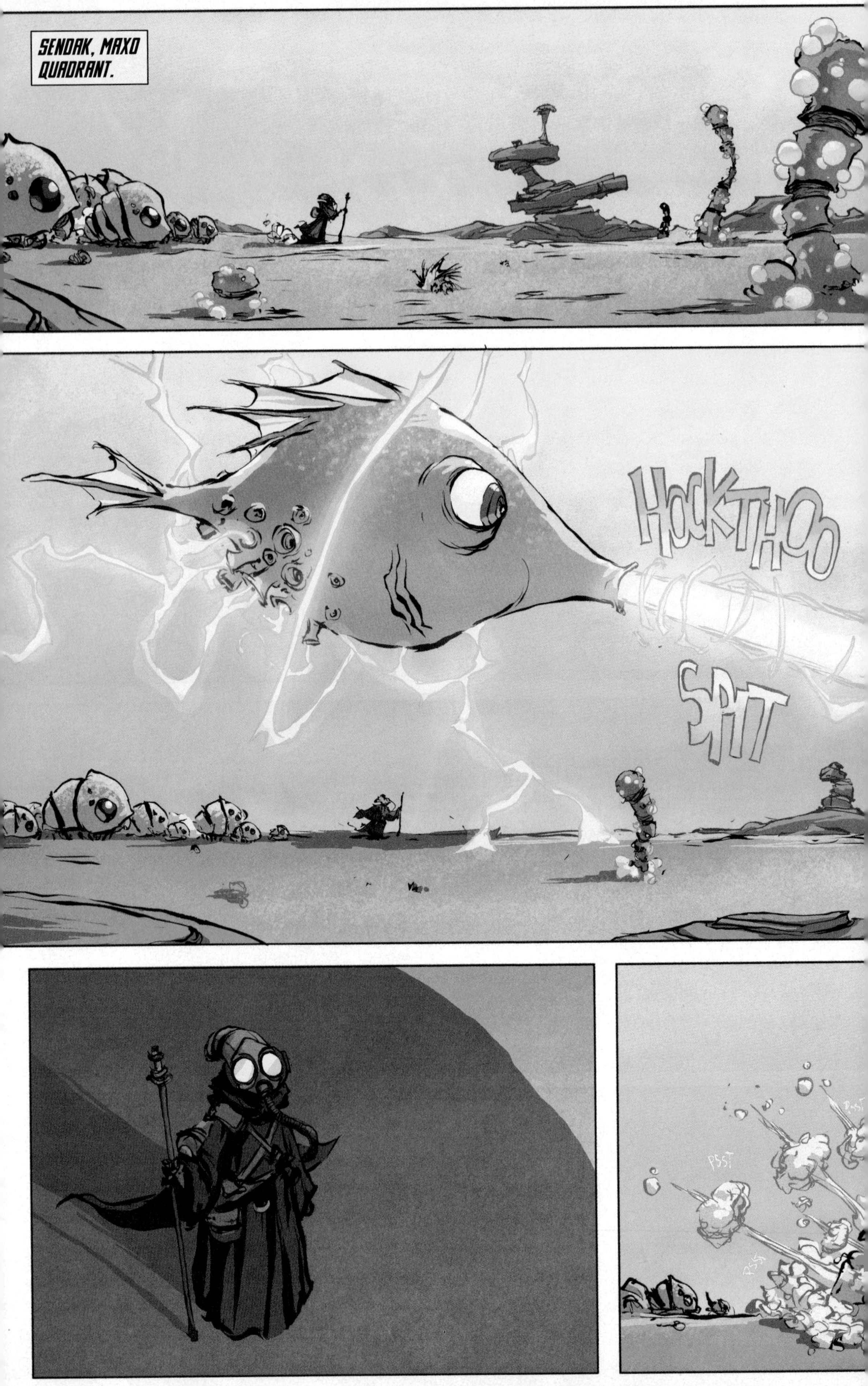
SENDAK, MAXO QUADRANT.
HOCKTHOO
SPIT
PSST
PSST
PSST

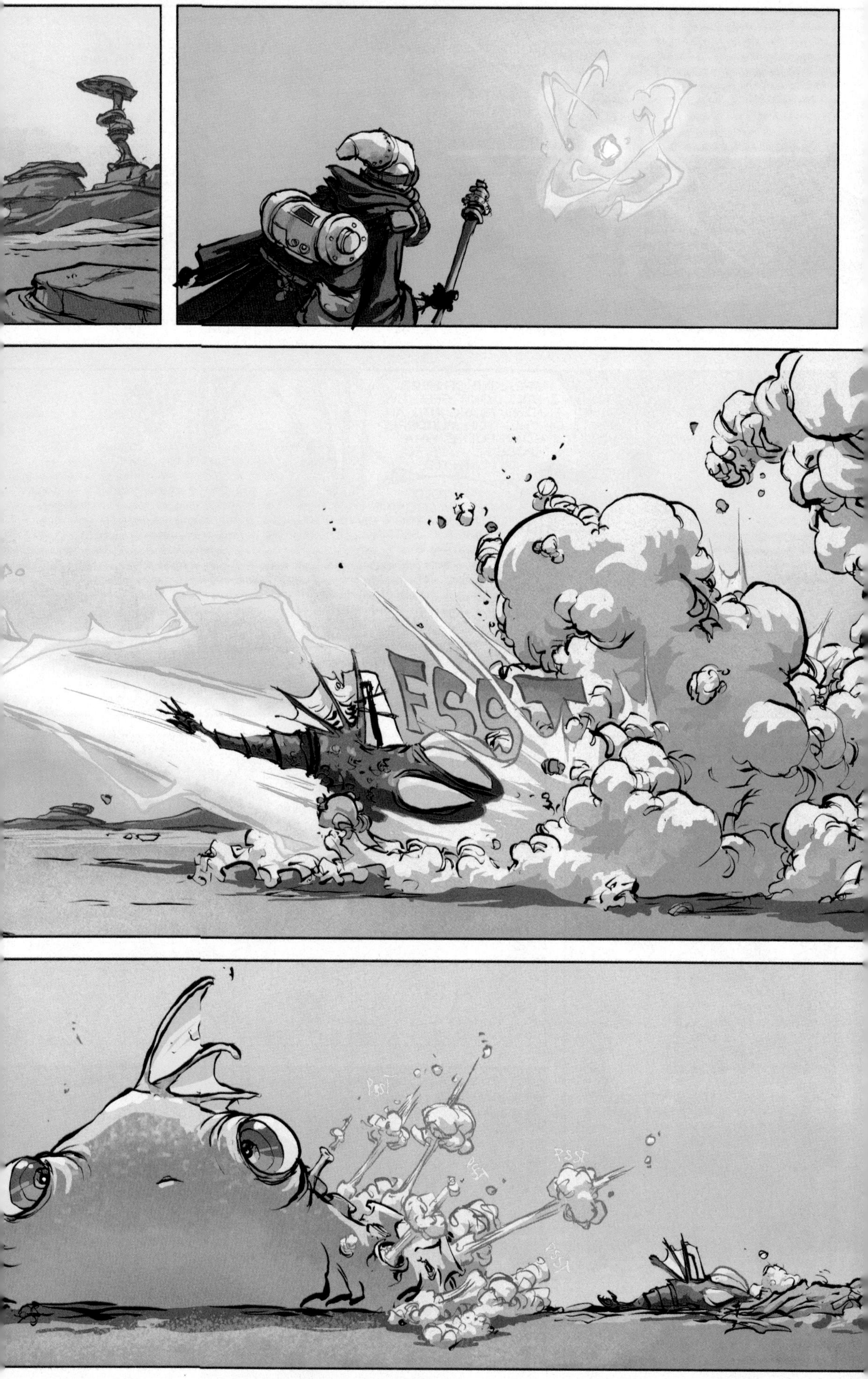
FSST
PSST
PSST
PSST
PSST

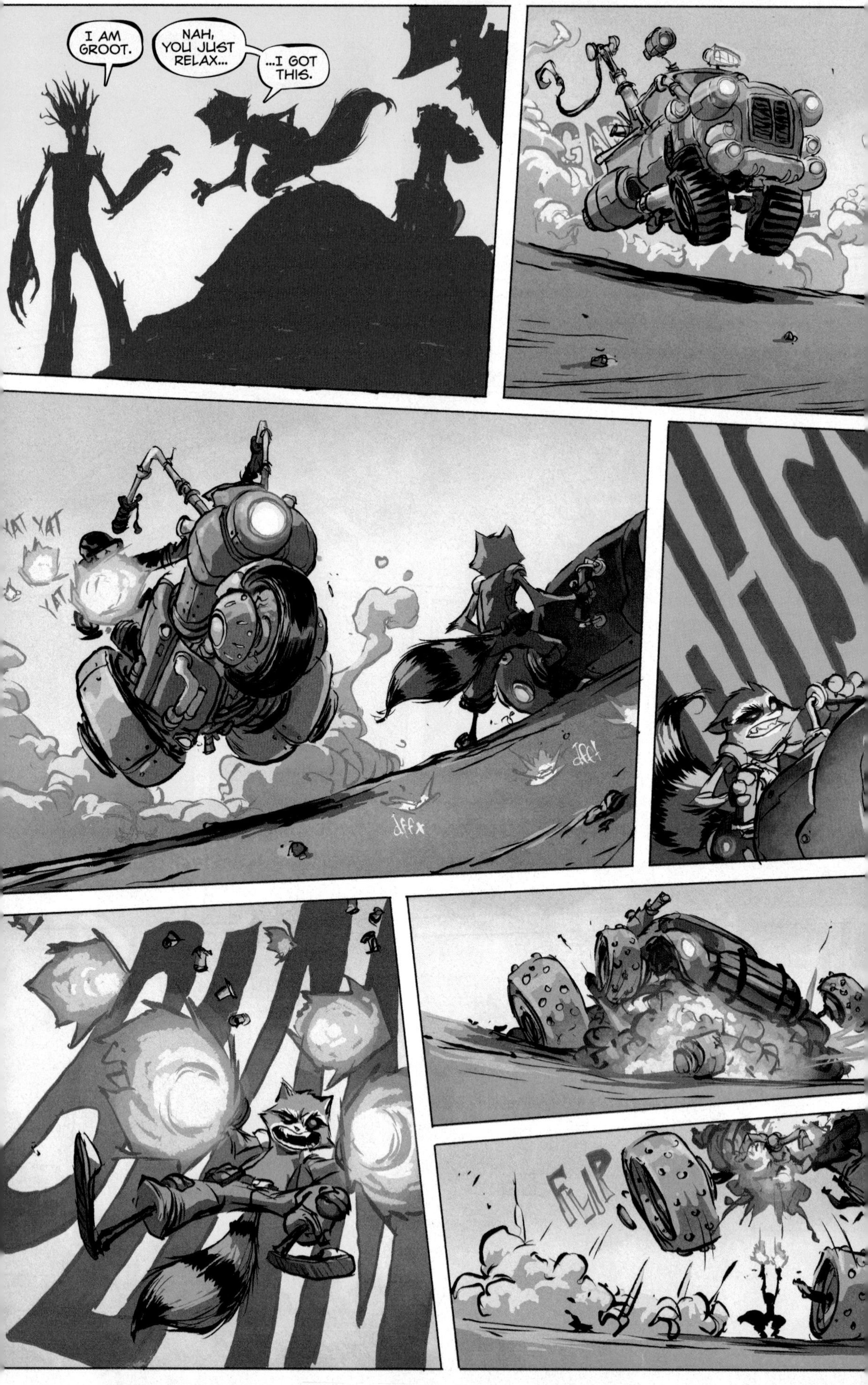
I AM GROOT.
NAH, YOU JUST RELAX...
...I GOT THIS.
YAT YAT
YAT
FLIP

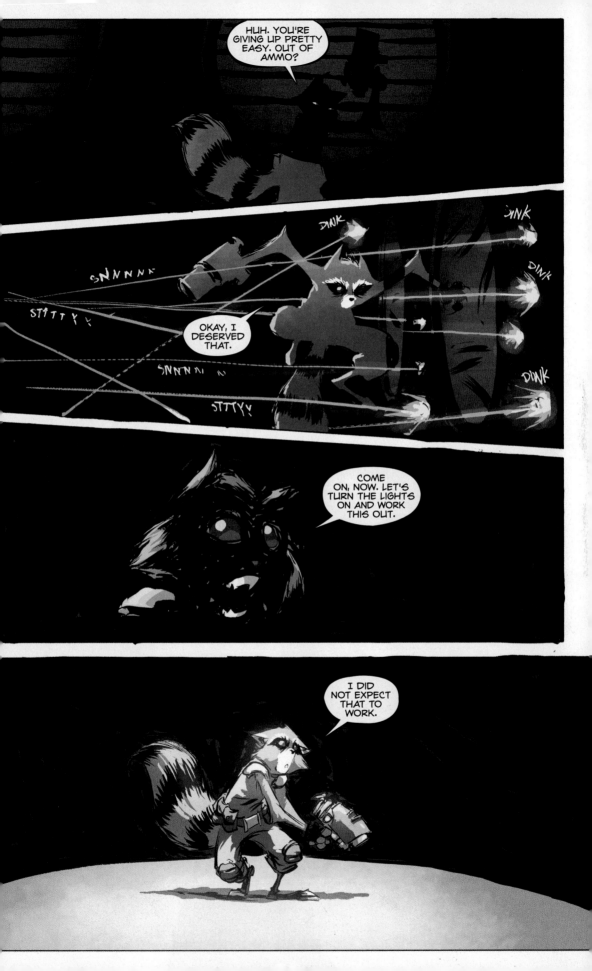

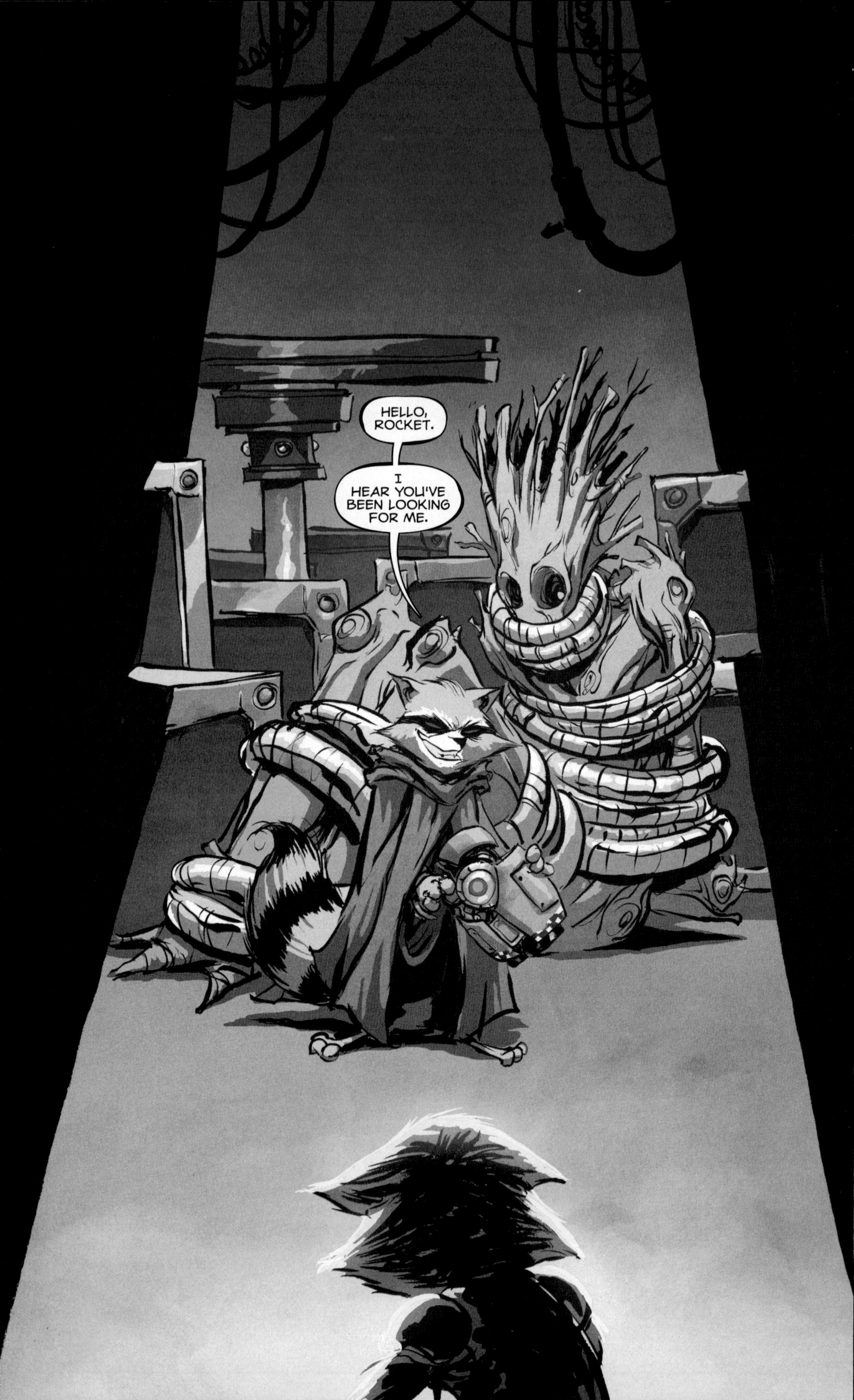
HELLO, ROCKET.
I HEAR YOU'VE BEEN LOOKING FOR ME.

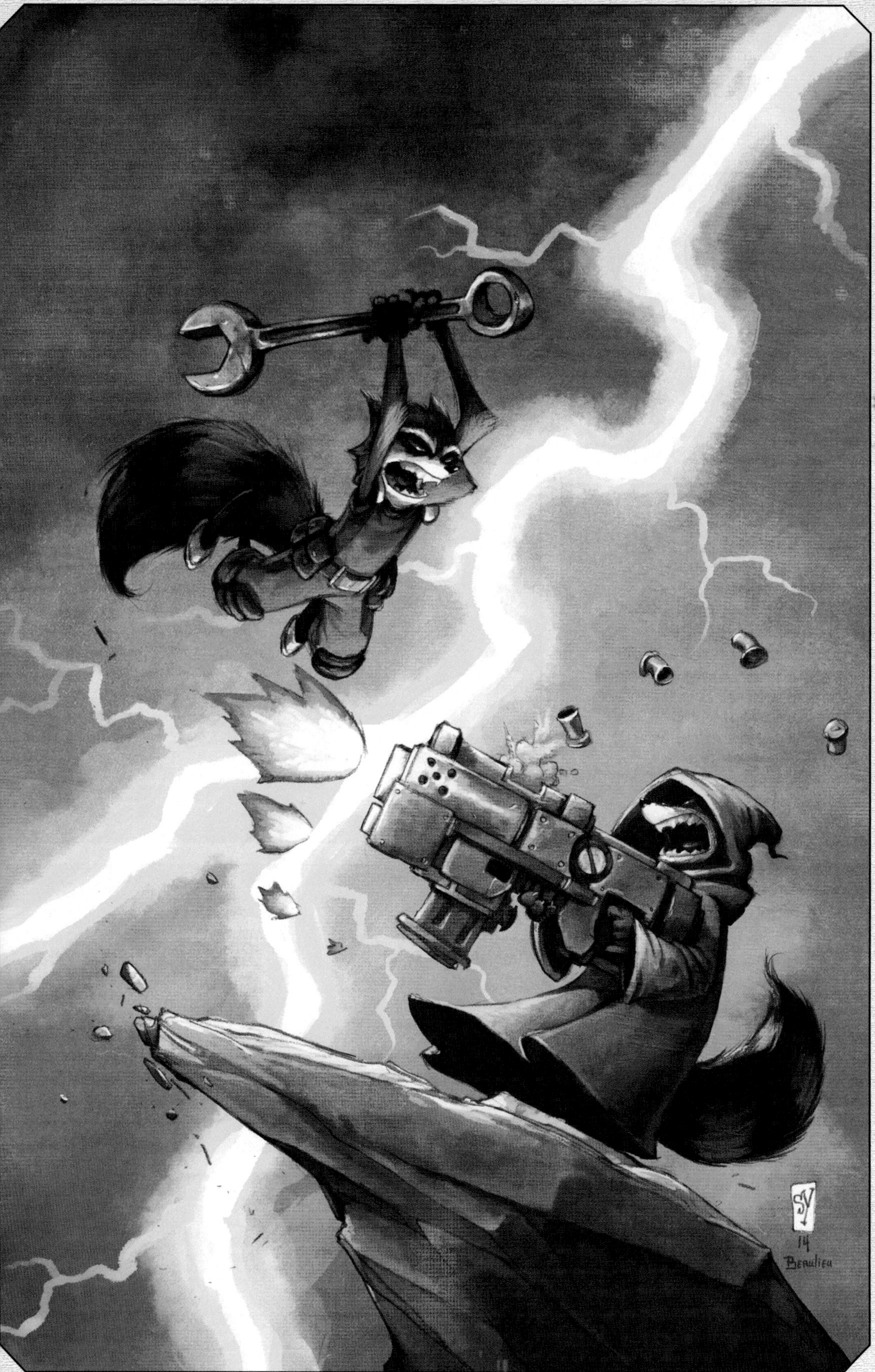
SY
14
Beaulieu

4

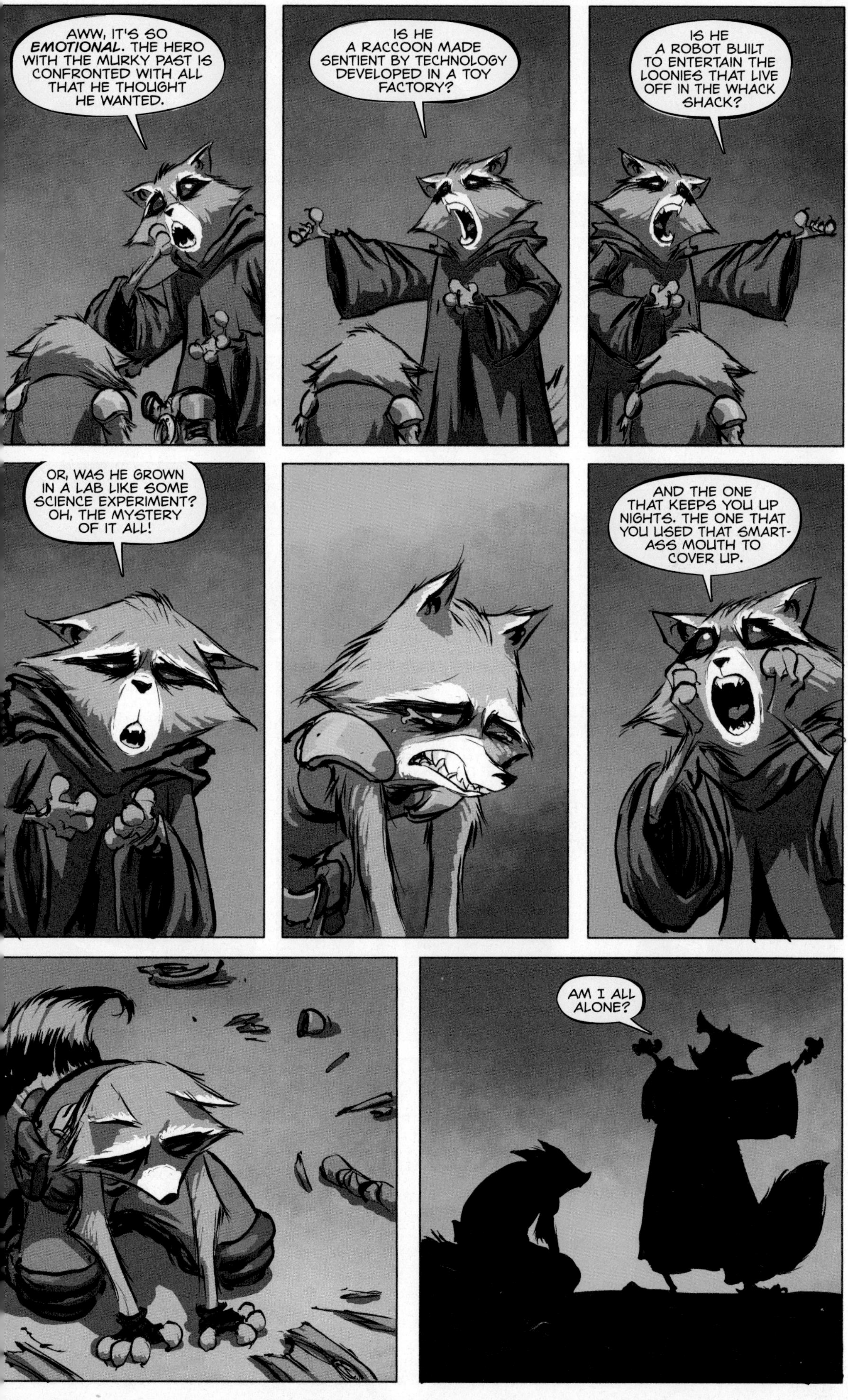
AWW, IT'S SO *EMOTIONAL*. THE HERO WITH THE MURKY PAST IS CONFRONTED WITH ALL THAT HE THOUGHT HE WANTED.
IS HE A RACCOON MADE SENTIENT BY TECHNOLOGY DEVELOPED IN A TOY FACTORY?
IS HE A ROBOT BUILT TO ENTERTAIN THE LOONIES THAT LIVE OFF IN THE WHACK SHACK?
OR, WAS HE GROWN IN A LAB LIKE SOME SCIENCE EXPERIMENT? OH, THE MYSTERY OF IT ALL!
AND THE ONE THAT KEEPS YOU UP NIGHTS. THE ONE THAT YOU USED THAT SMART-ASS MOUTH TO COVER UP.
AM I ALL ALONE?

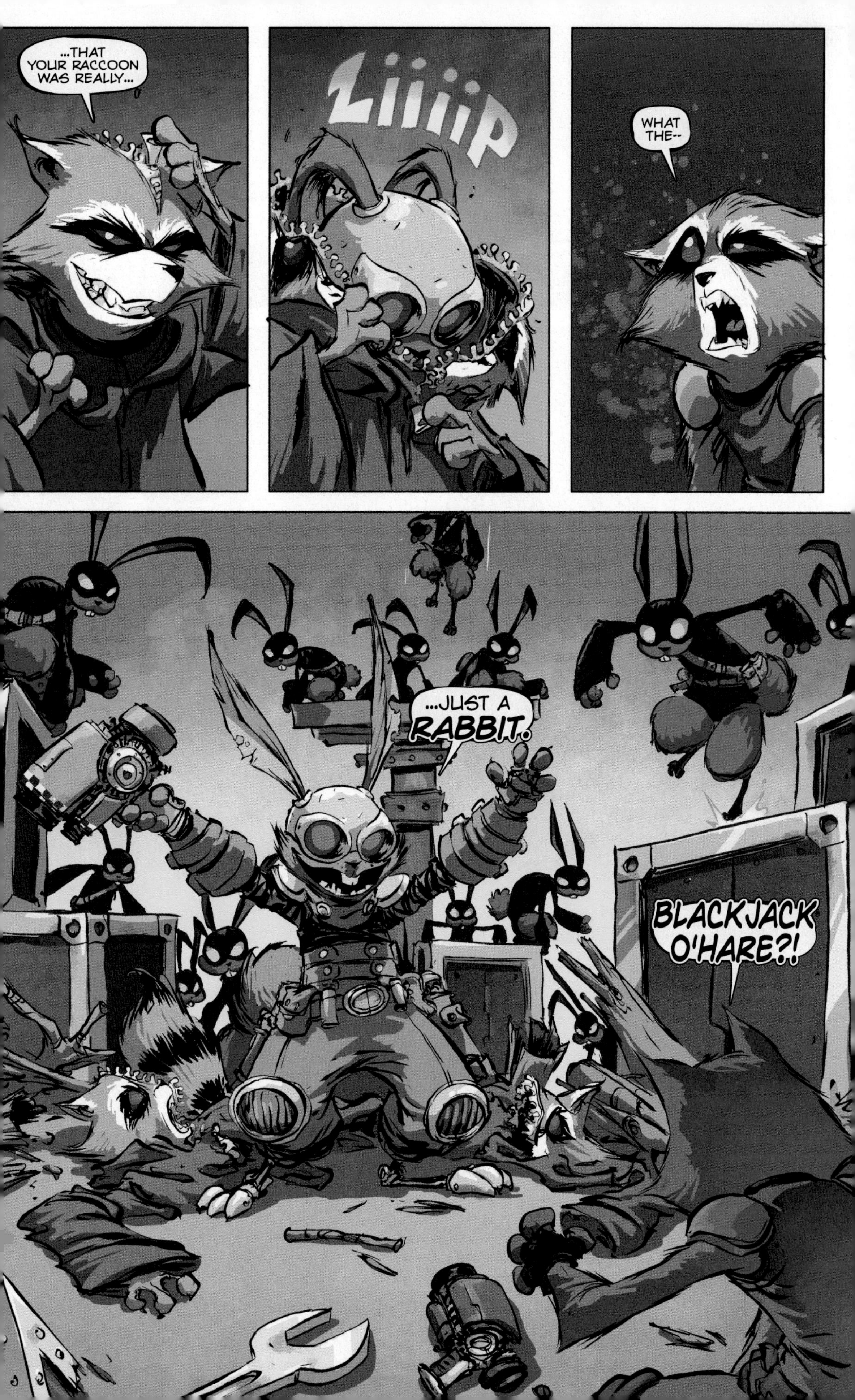
...THAT YOUR RACCOON WAS REALLY...
LIIIIP
WHAT THE--
...JUST A RABBIT.
BLACKJACK O'HARE?!

ARE YOU KIDDING ME? *YOU'VE* BEEN BEHIND ALL THIS?

WHAT DID I EVER DO TO YOU?

KRAK!

THREE YEARS AGO I HAD A JOB. THE *BIG* ONE.

NOW I GOTTA RELAX

"IT WAS EASY. TAKE OUT THE MARK AND I COULD PACK IT IN. RETIRE TO A BEACH SOMEWHERE ON LEXO OR BELLYION."

ZOO'OOO'OOO

"IT WAS SUPPOSED TO GO SMOOTH. BREAK IN. TAKE OUT TWO GUARDS AND POP, ONE LESS PRINCESS IN THE GALAXY."

"BUT SOMEONE WAS THERE BEFORE ME."

SMOOCH!!

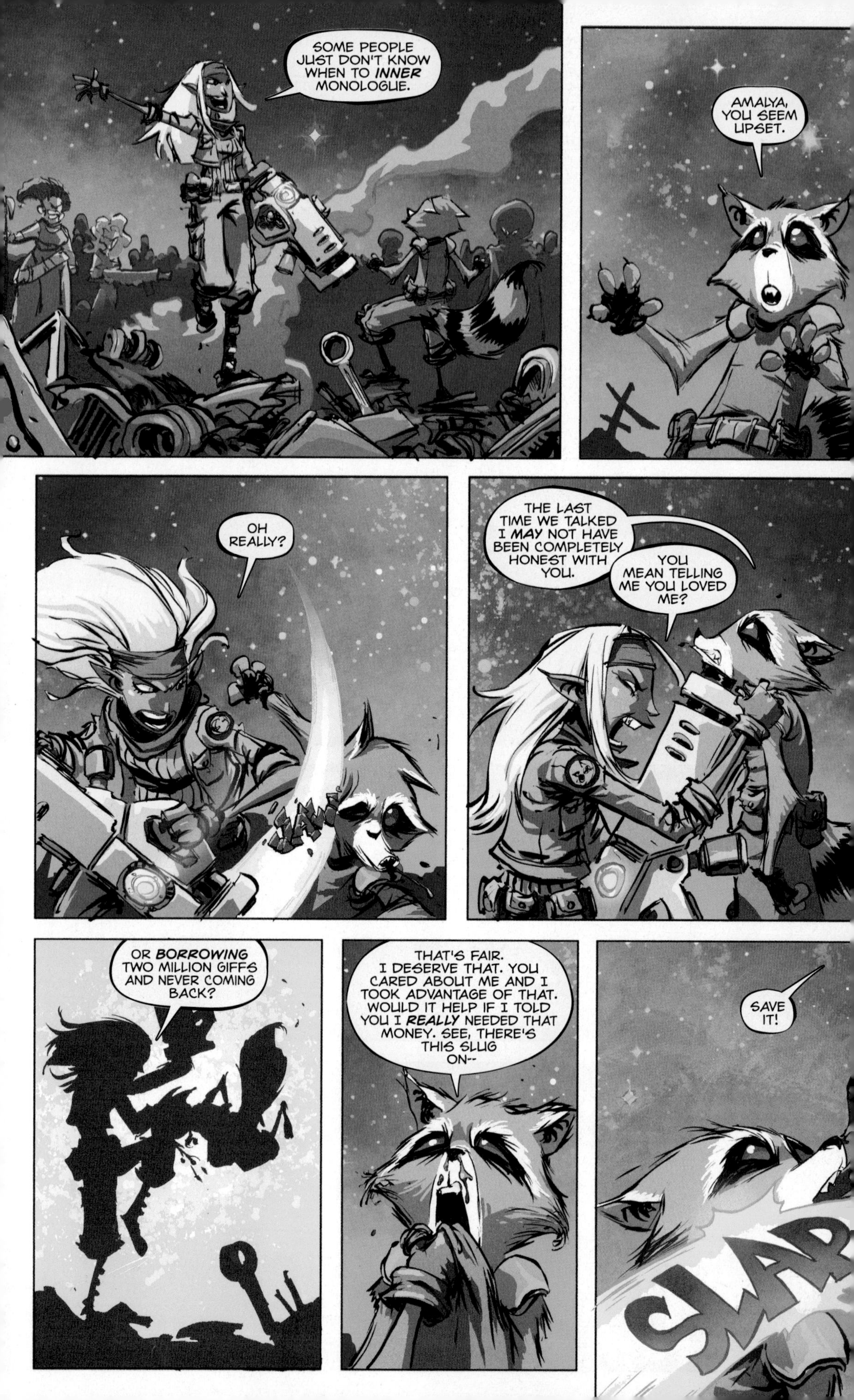
SOME PEOPLE JUST DON'T KNOW WHEN TO INNER MONOLOGUE.
AMALYA, YOU SEEM UPSET.
OH REALLY?
THE LAST TIME WE TALKED I MAY NOT HAVE BEEN COMPLETELY HONEST WITH YOU.
YOU MEAN TELLING ME YOU LOVED ME?
OR BORROWING TWO MILLION GIFFS AND NEVER COMING BACK?
THAT'S FAIR. I DESERVE THAT. YOU CARED ABOUT ME AND I TOOK ADVANTAGE OF THAT. WOULD IT HELP IF I TOLD YOU I REALLY NEEDED THAT MONEY. SEE, THERE'S THIS SLUG ON--
SAVE IT!

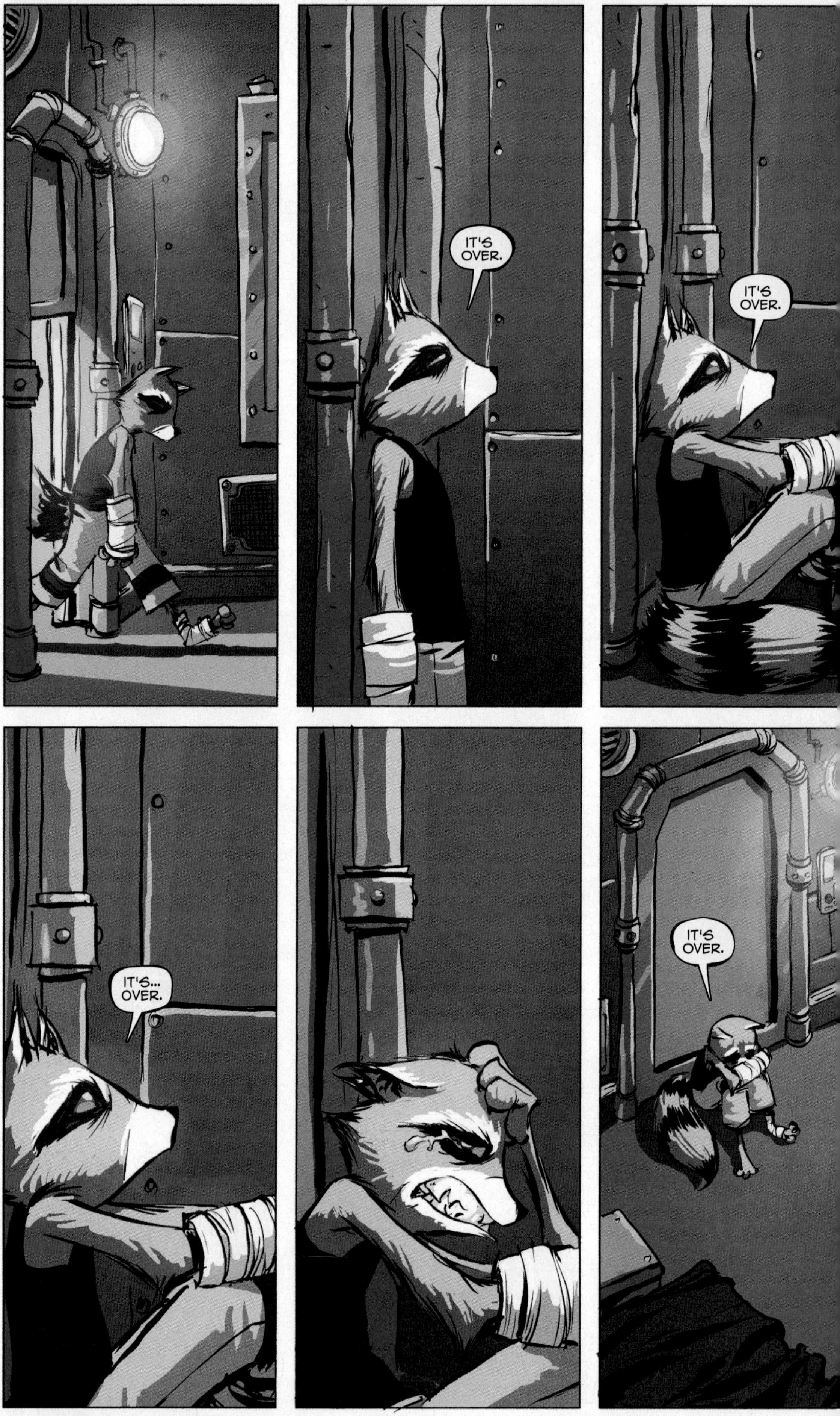
IT'S OVER.
IT'S OVER.
IT'S... OVER.
IT'S OVER.

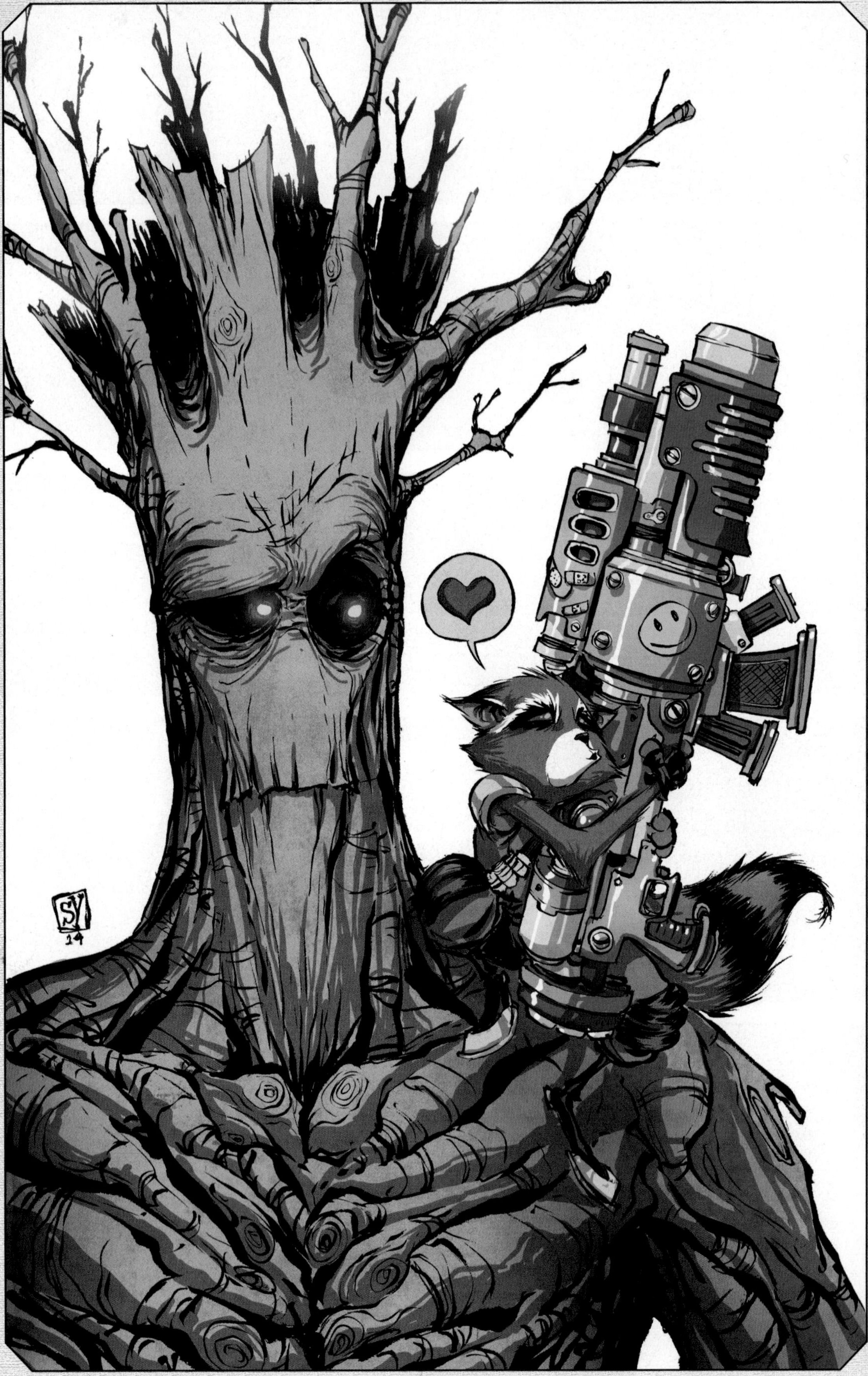
SY
14

5

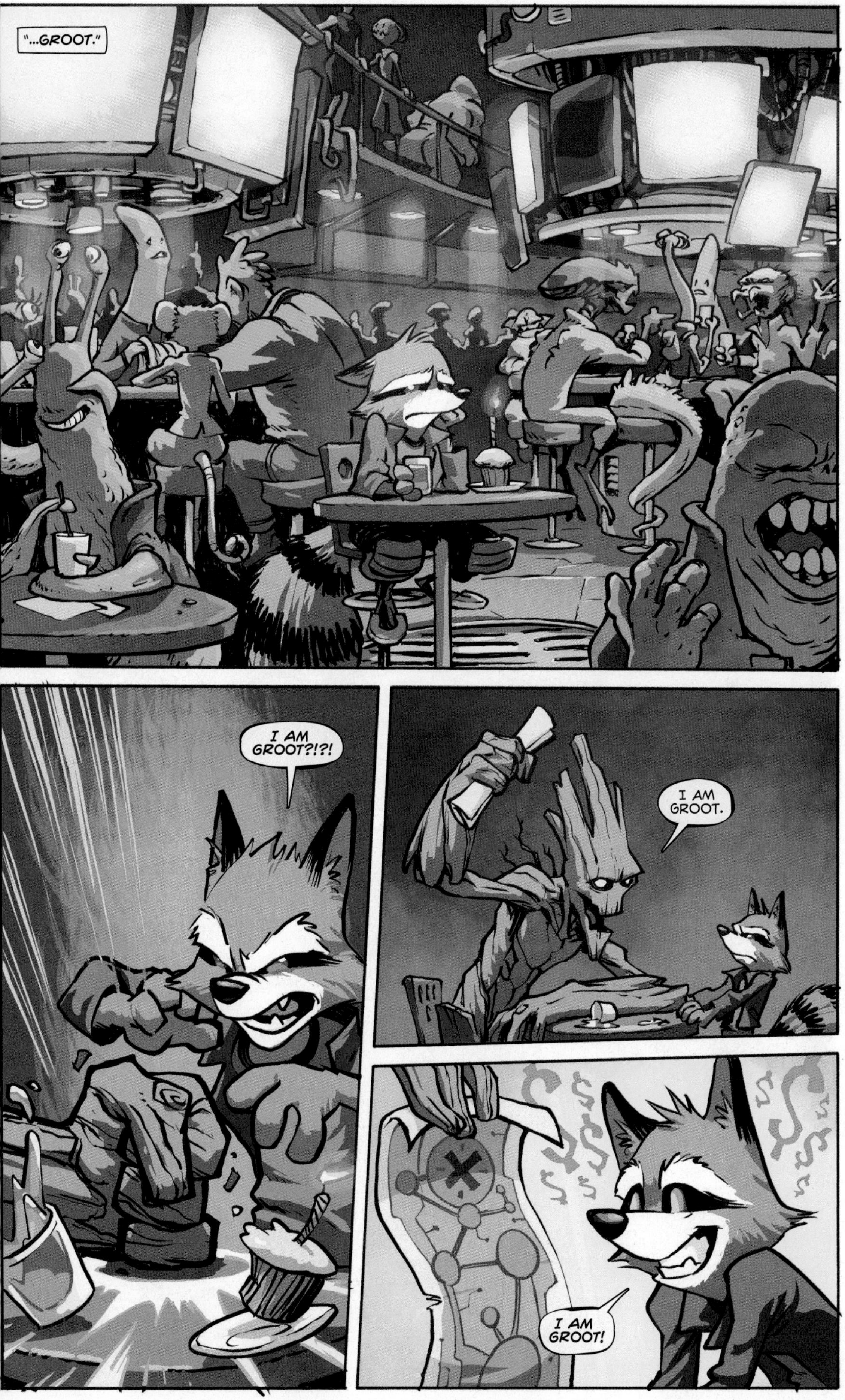
"...GROOT."
I AM GROOT?!?!
I AM GROOT.
I AM GROOT!

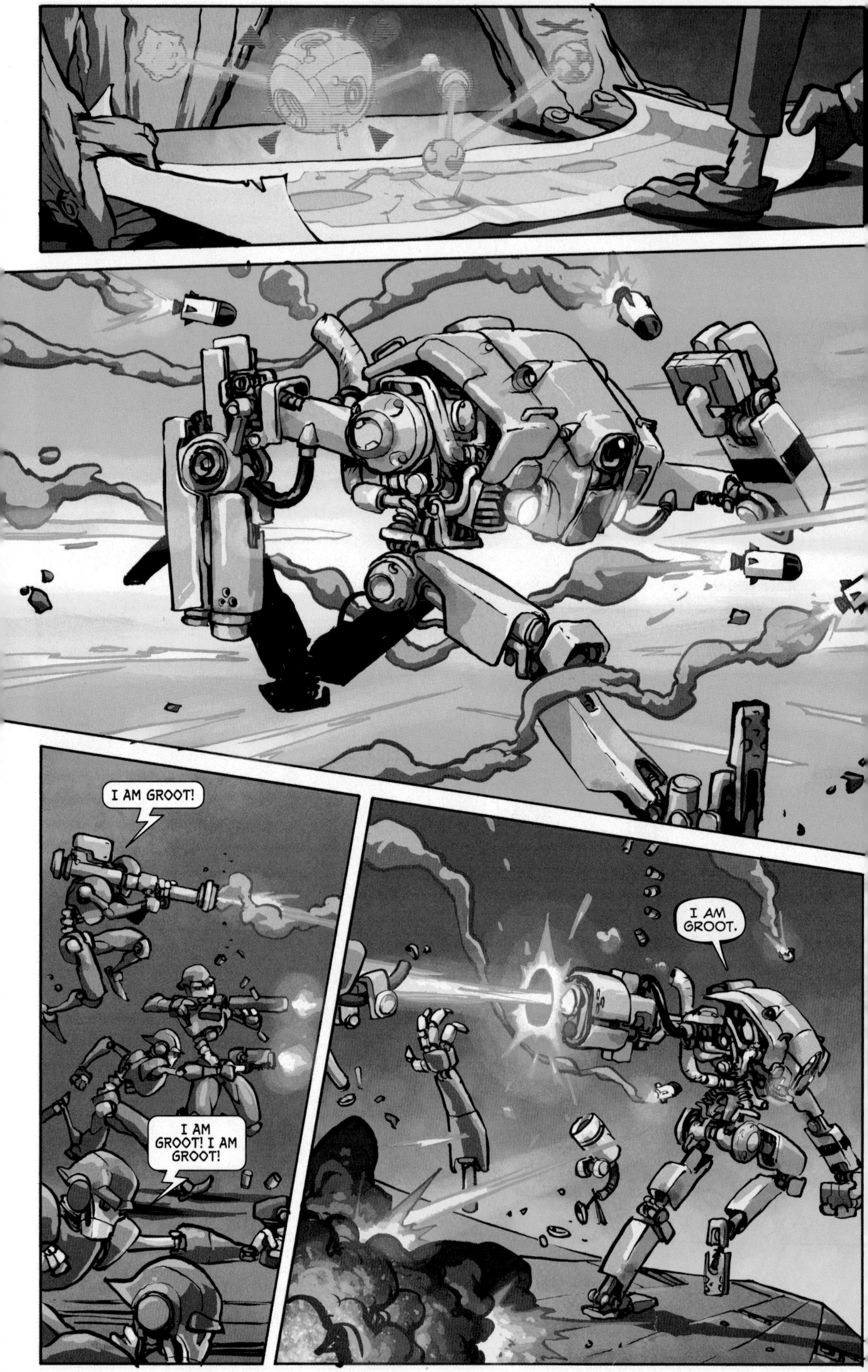
I AM GROOT!
I AM GROOT! I AM GROOT!
I AM GROOT.

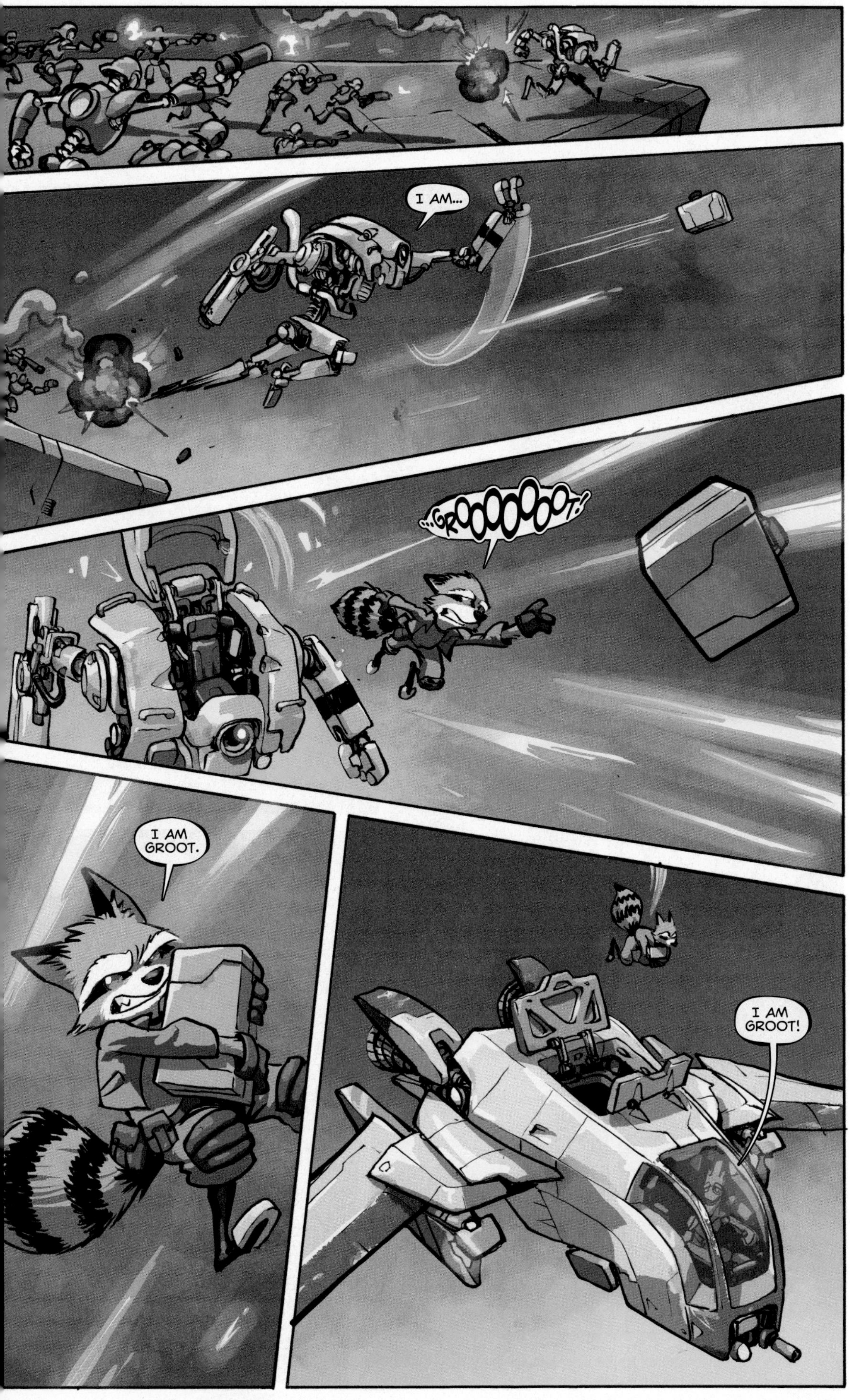
I AM...
...GROOOOOOOOT!
I AM GROOT.
I AM GROOT!

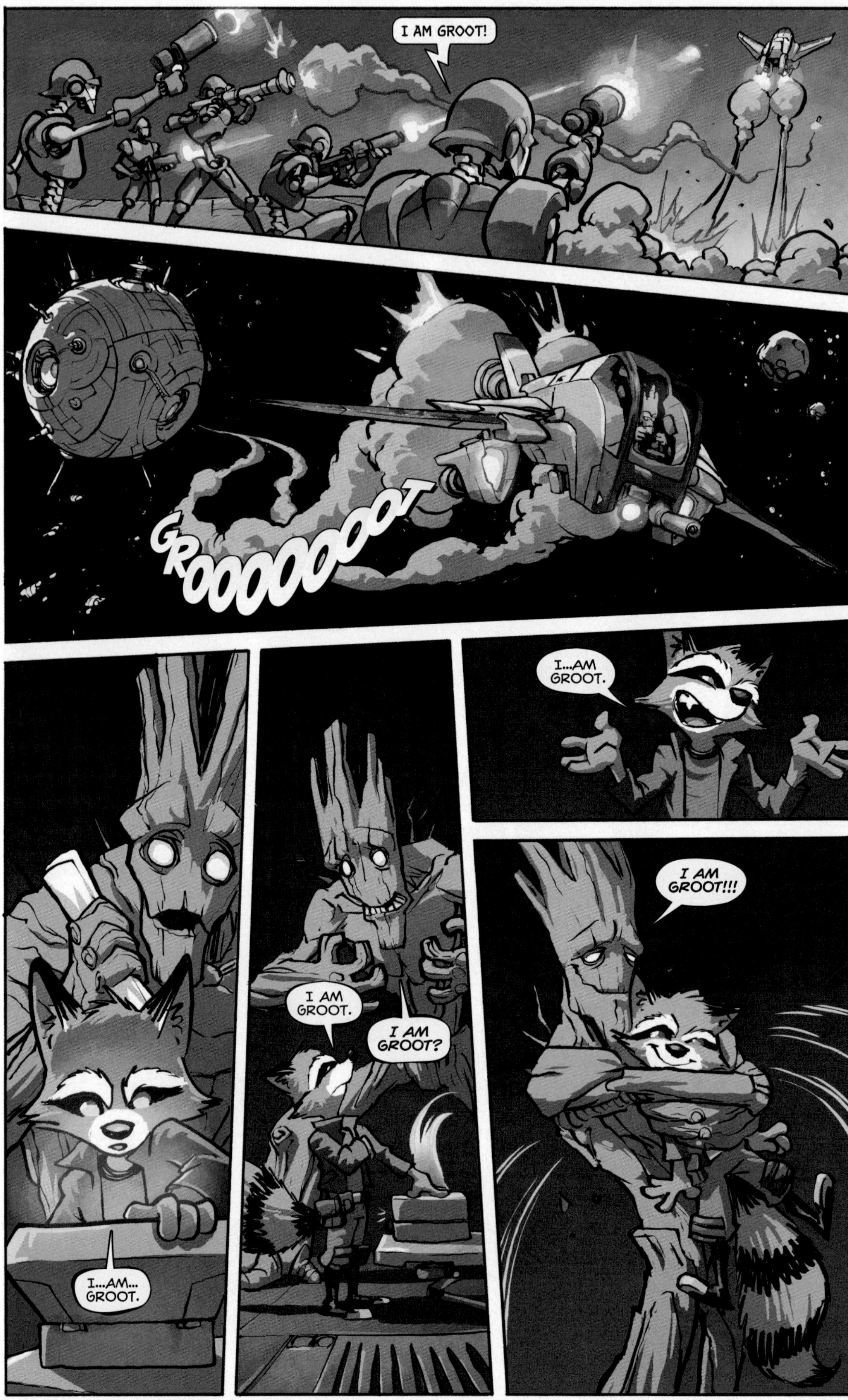
I AM GROOT!
GROOOOOOOOT
I...AM... GROOT.
I AM GROOT.
I AM GROOT?
I...AM GROOT.
I AM GROOT!!!

I AM GROOT,
I AM GROOT.

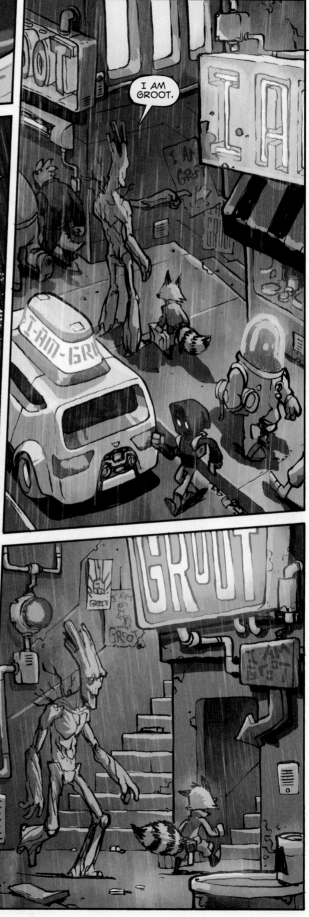

I AM
GROOT.

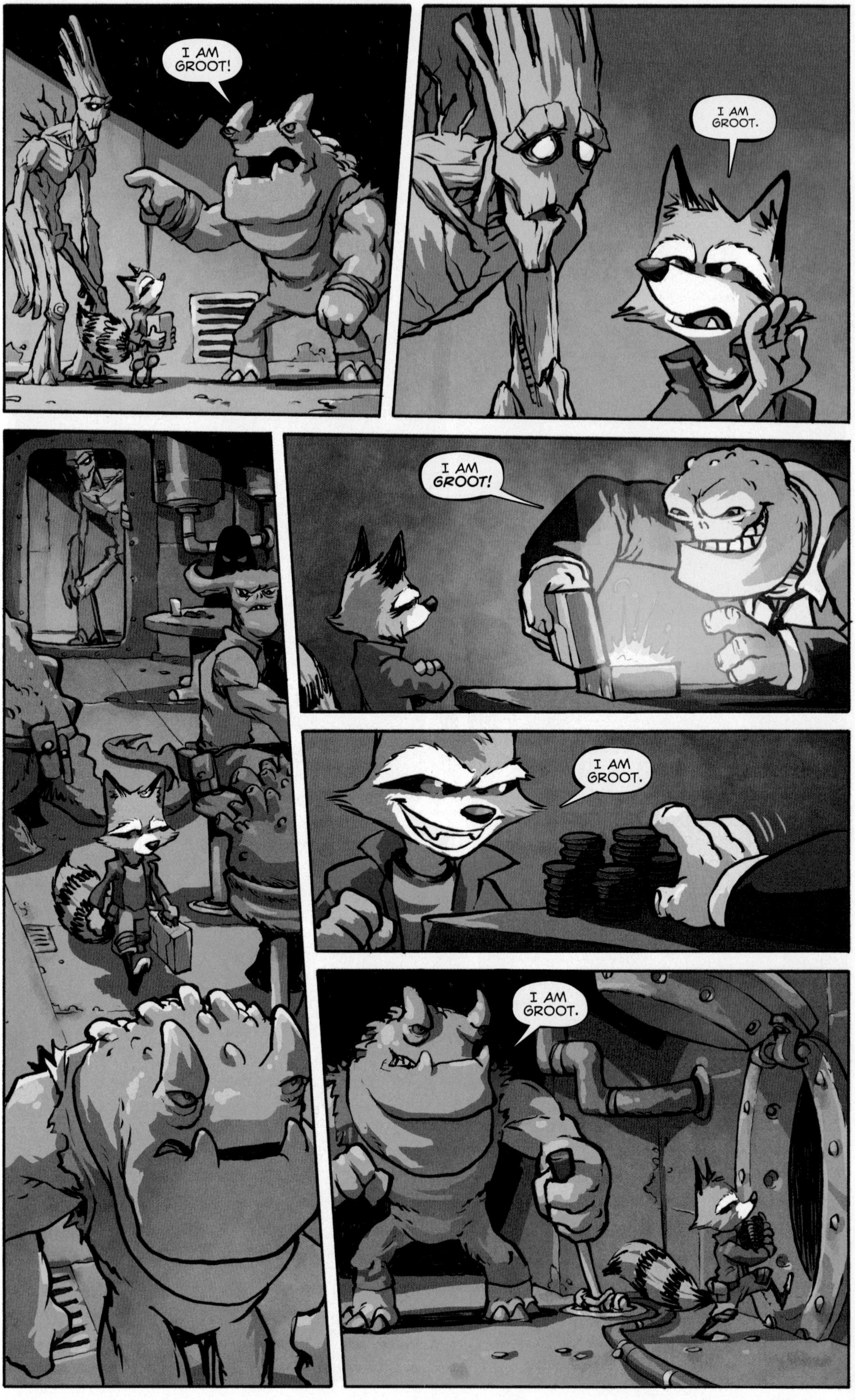
I AM GROOT!
I AM GROOT.
I AM GROOT!
I AM GROOT.
I AM GROOT.

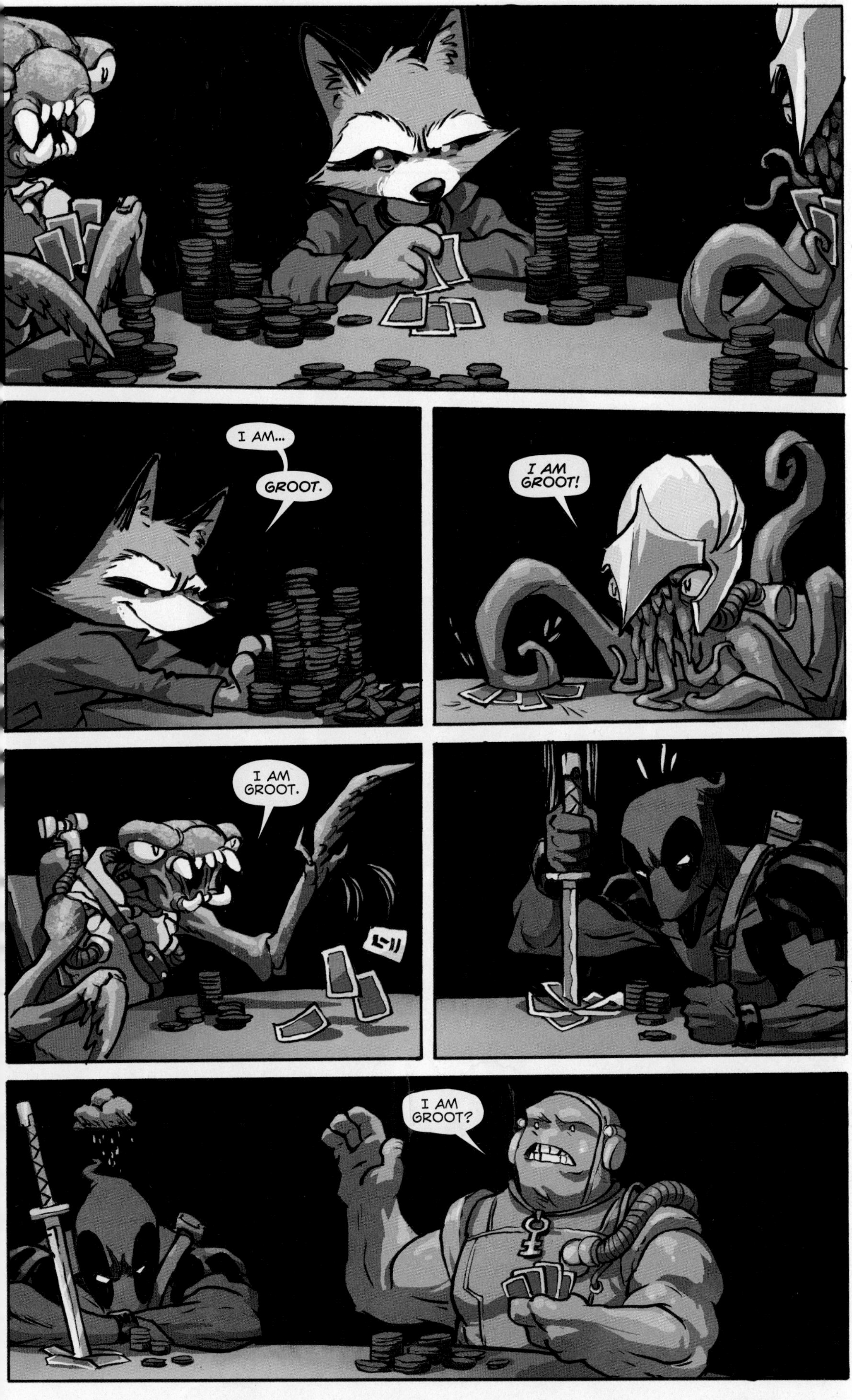
I AM...
GROOT.
I AM GROOT!
I AM GROOT.
I AM GROOT?

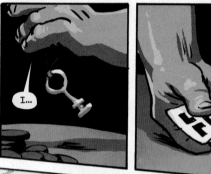

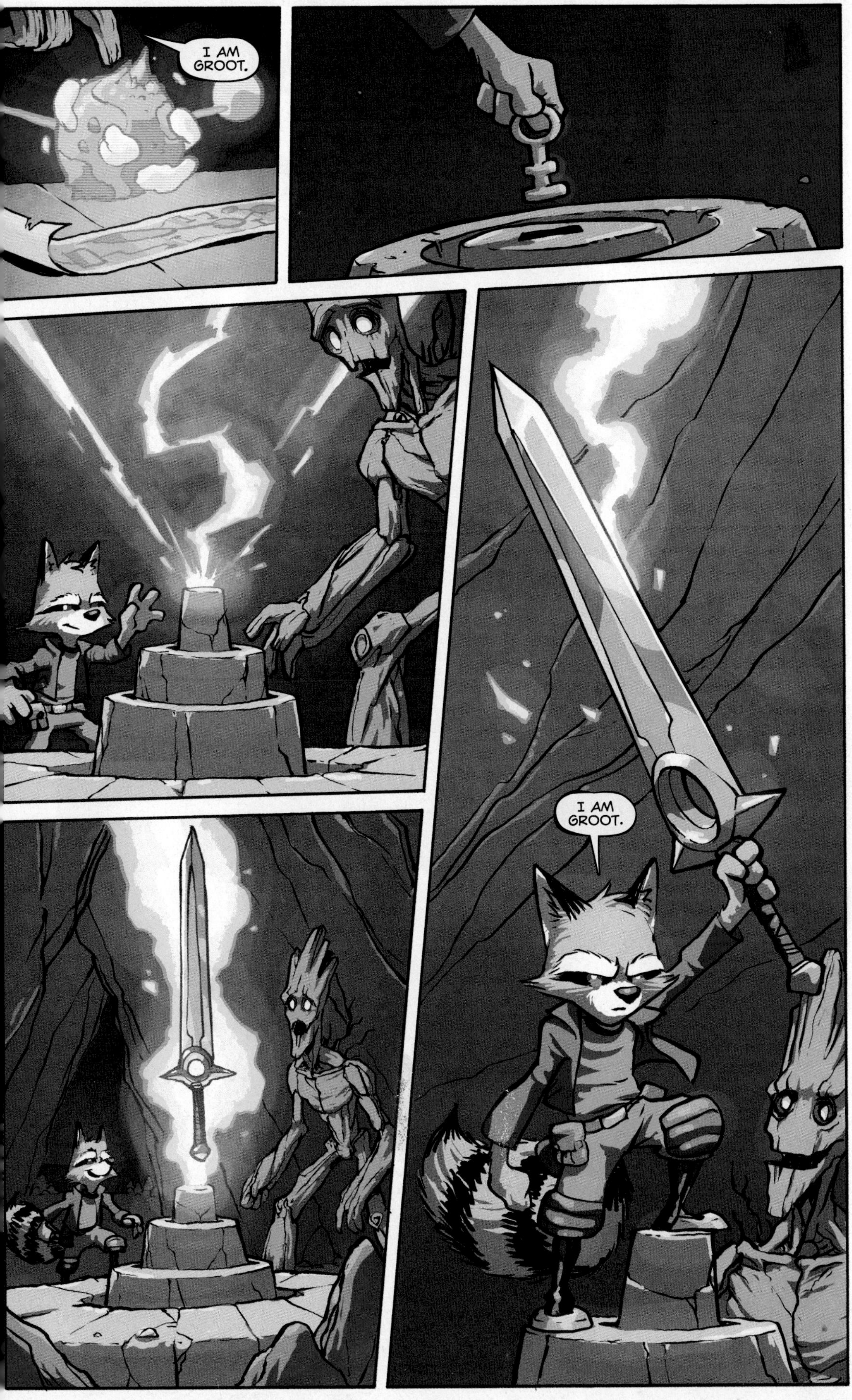
I AM GROOT.
I AM GROOT.

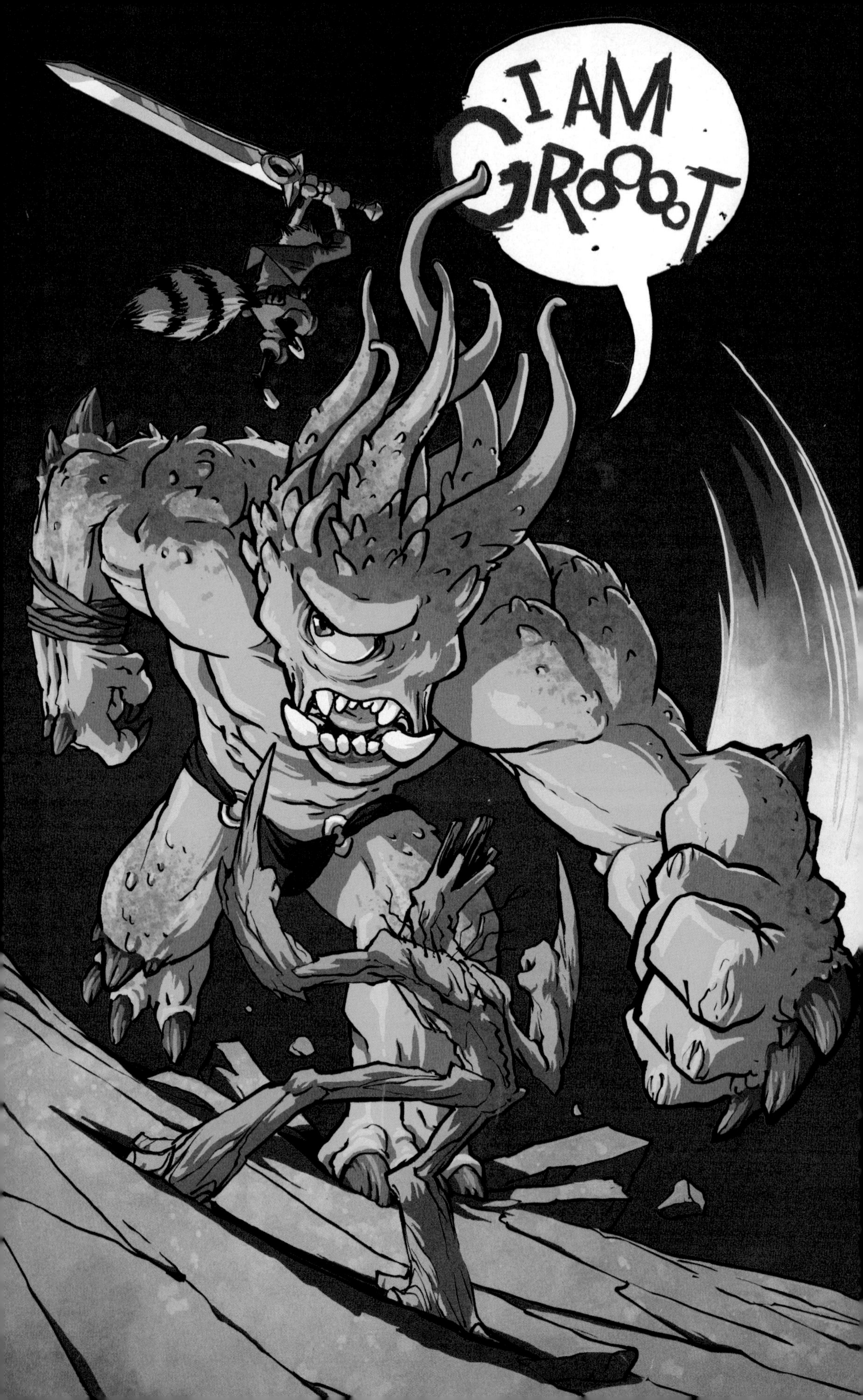
I AM GROOOOT

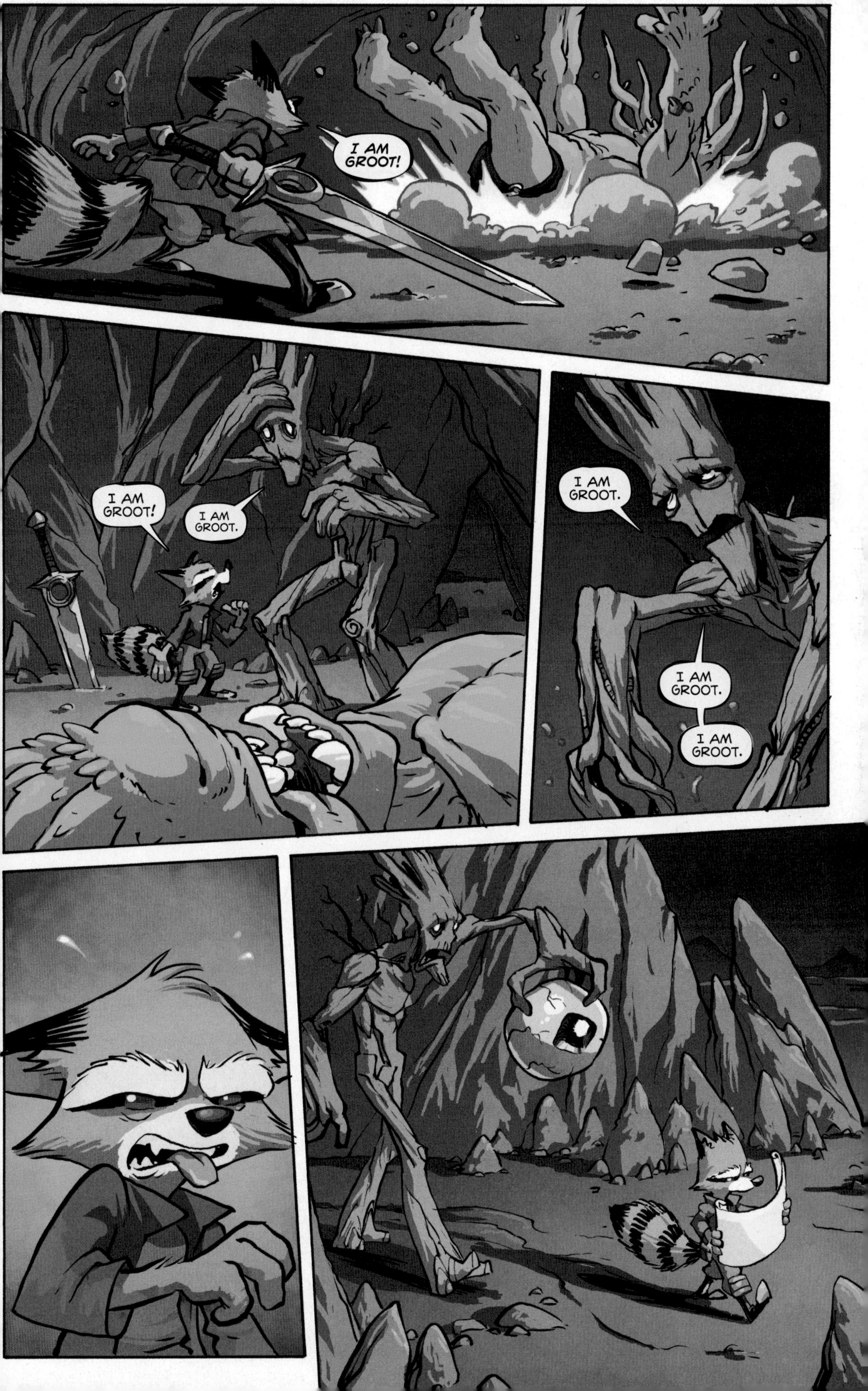
I AM GROOT!
I AM GROOT!
I AM GROOT.
I AM GROOT.
I AM GROOT.
I AM GROOT.

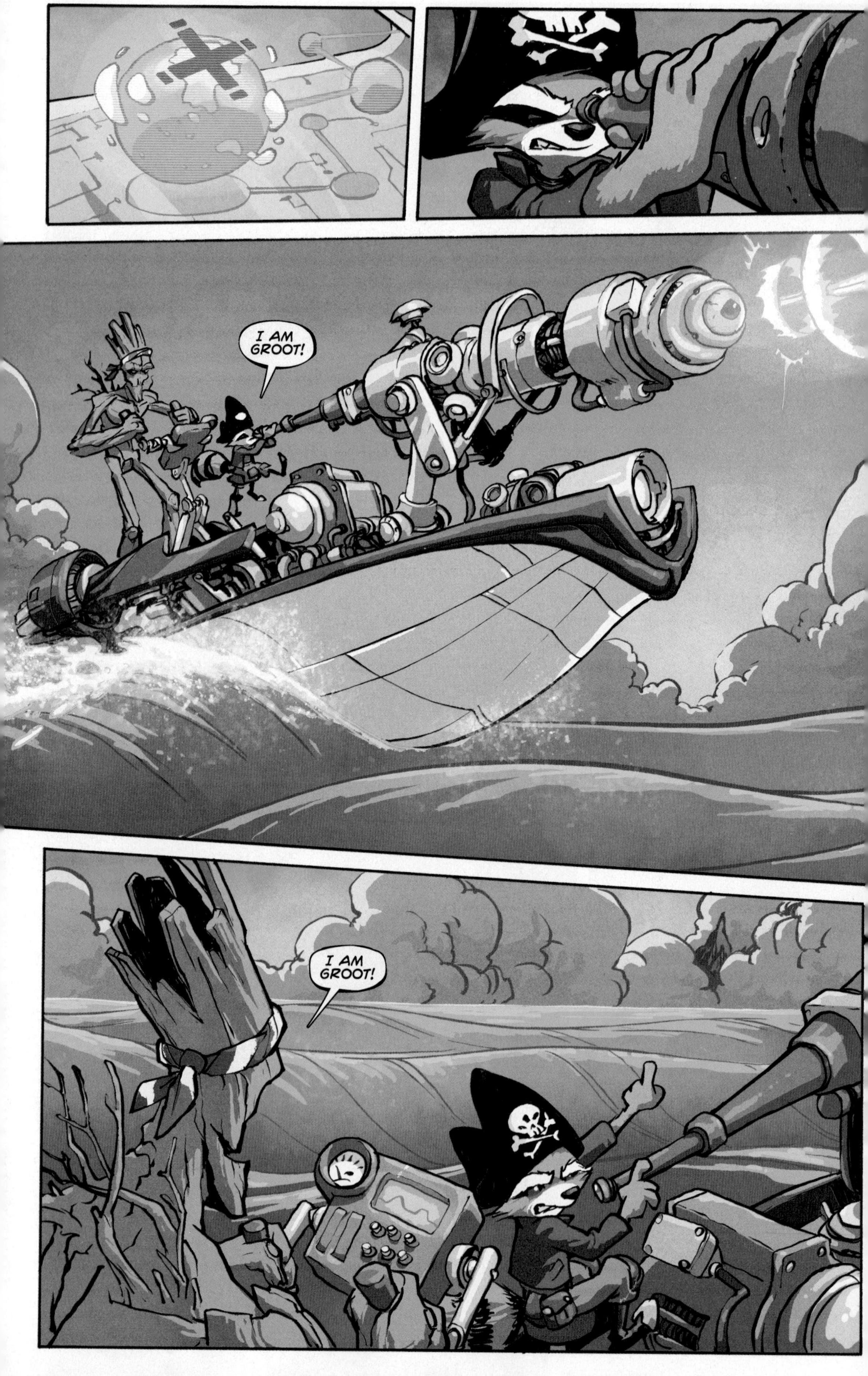
I AM GROOT!
I AM GROOT!

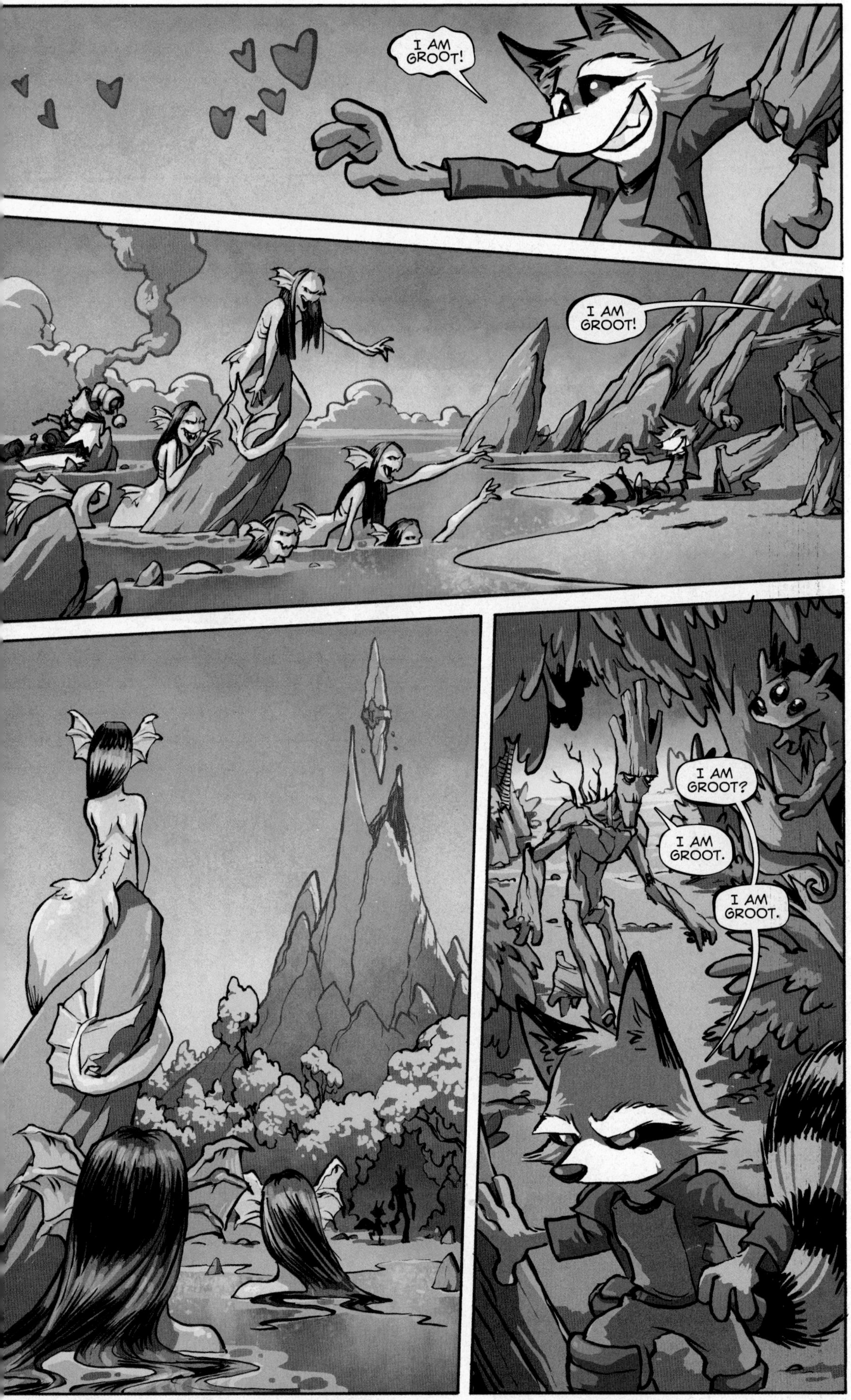
I AM GROOT!
I AM GROOT!
I AM GROOT?
I AM GROOT.
I AM GROOT.

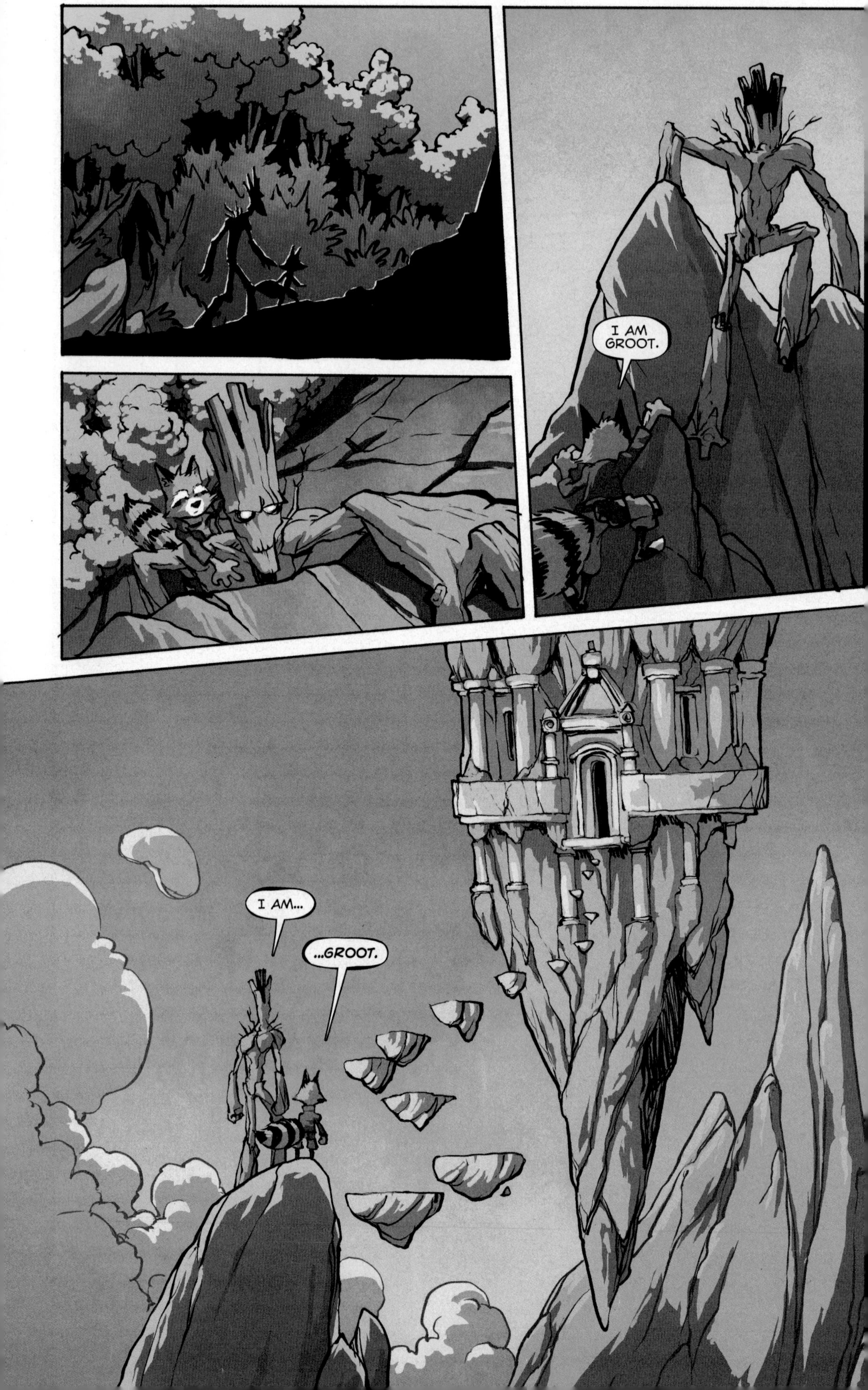
I AM GROOT.
I AM...
...GROOT.

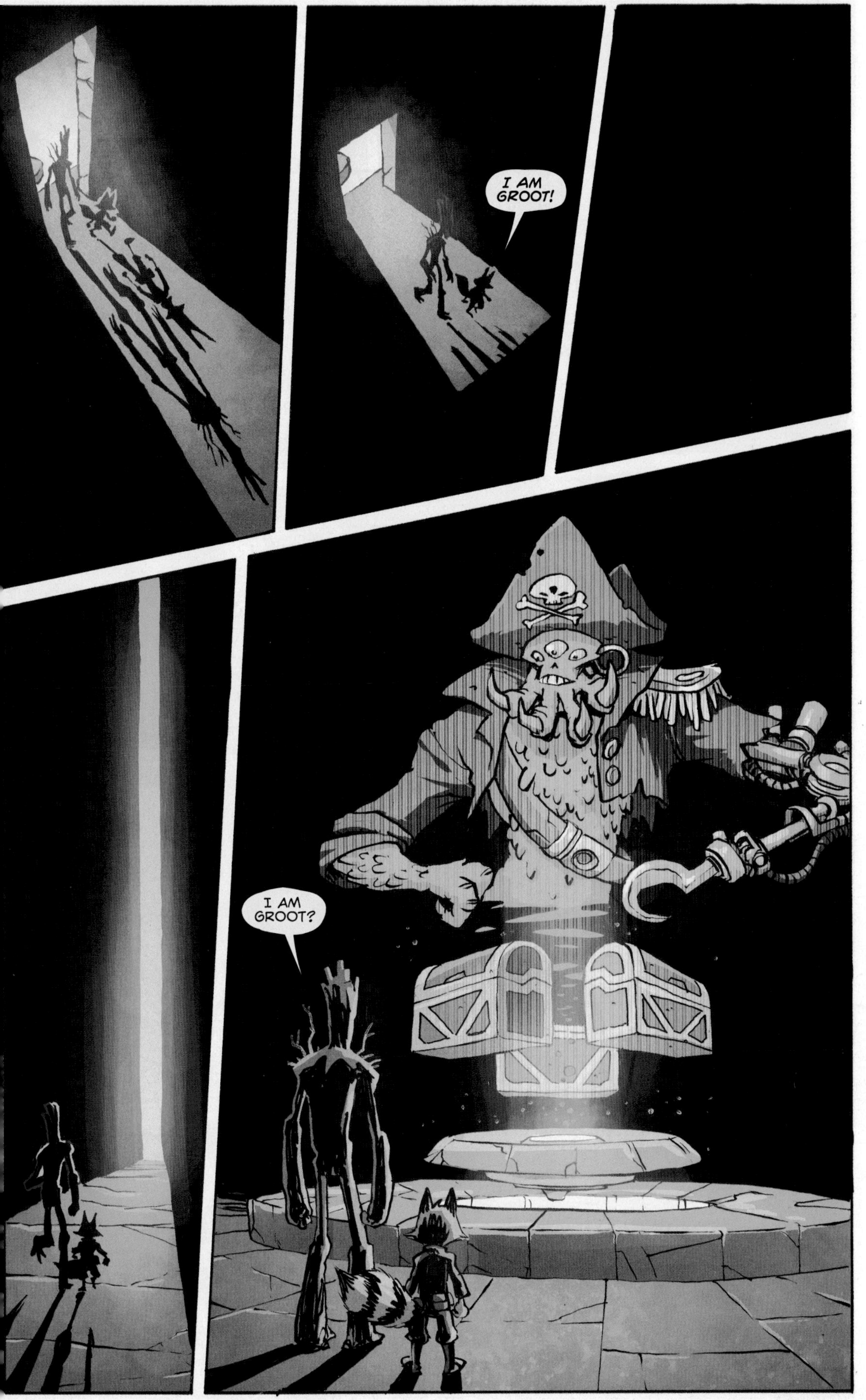
I AM GROOT!
I AM GROOT?

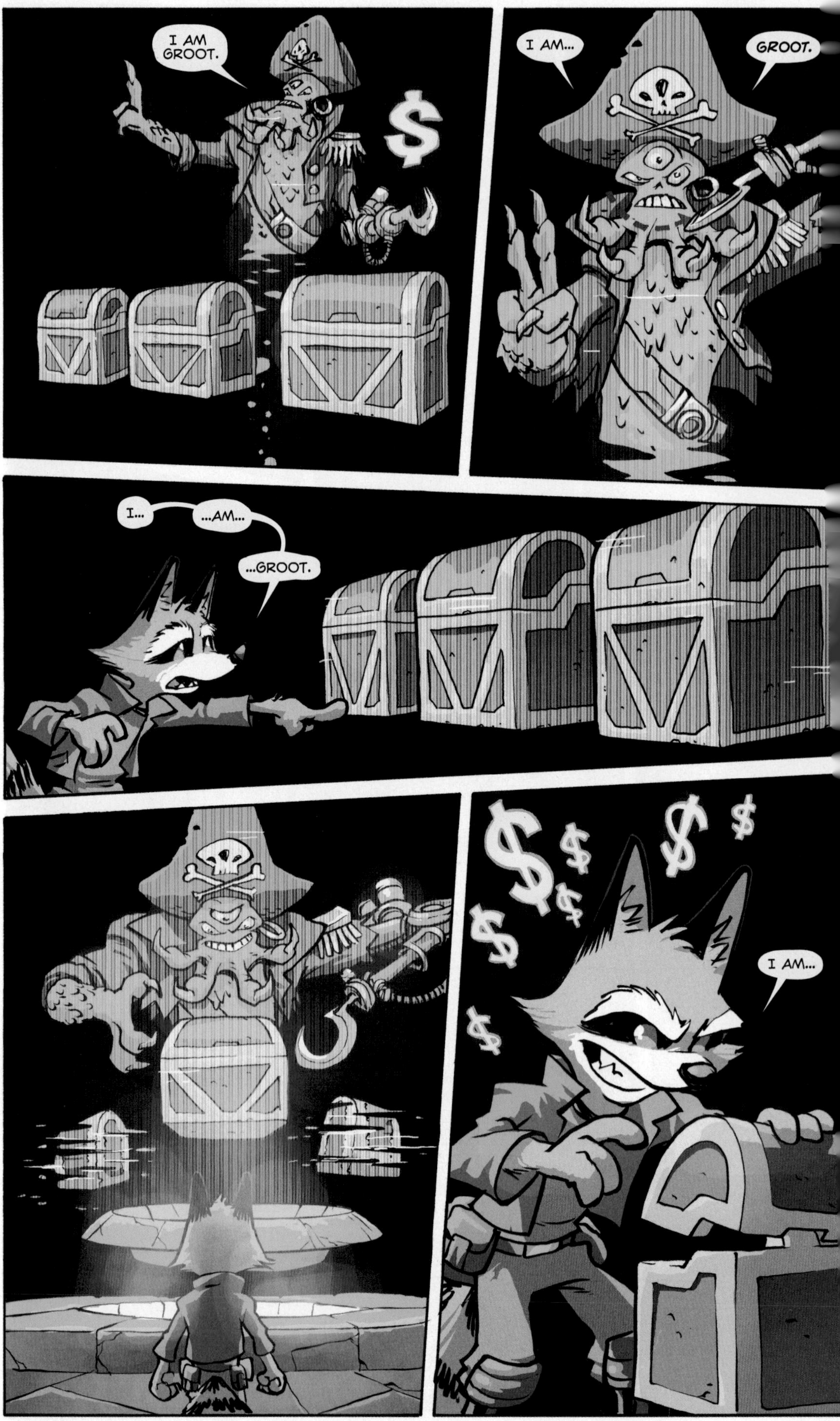
I AM GROOT.
I AM...
GROOT.
I...
...AM...
...GROOT.
I AM...

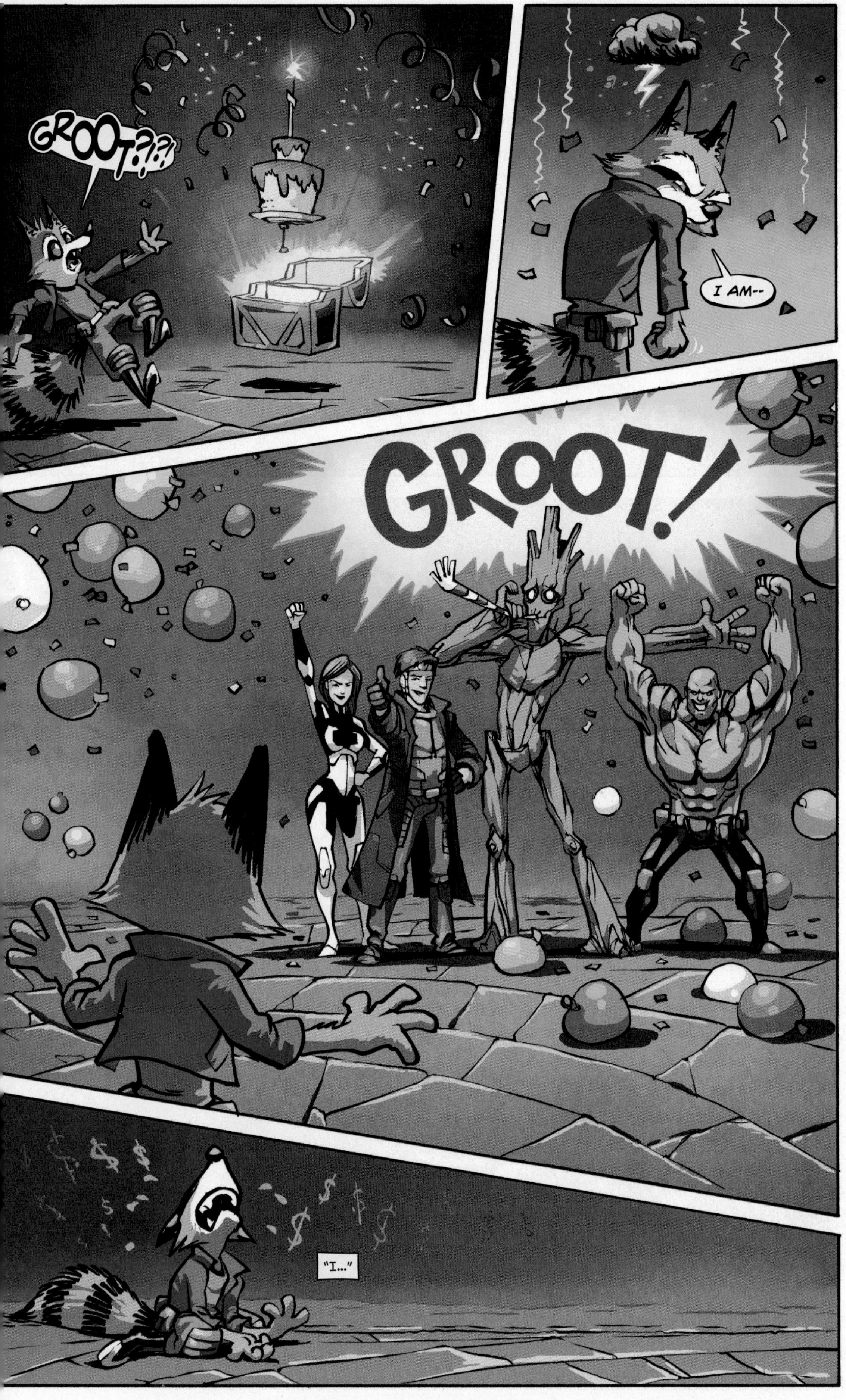
GROOT?!?!
I AM--
GROOT!
"I..."

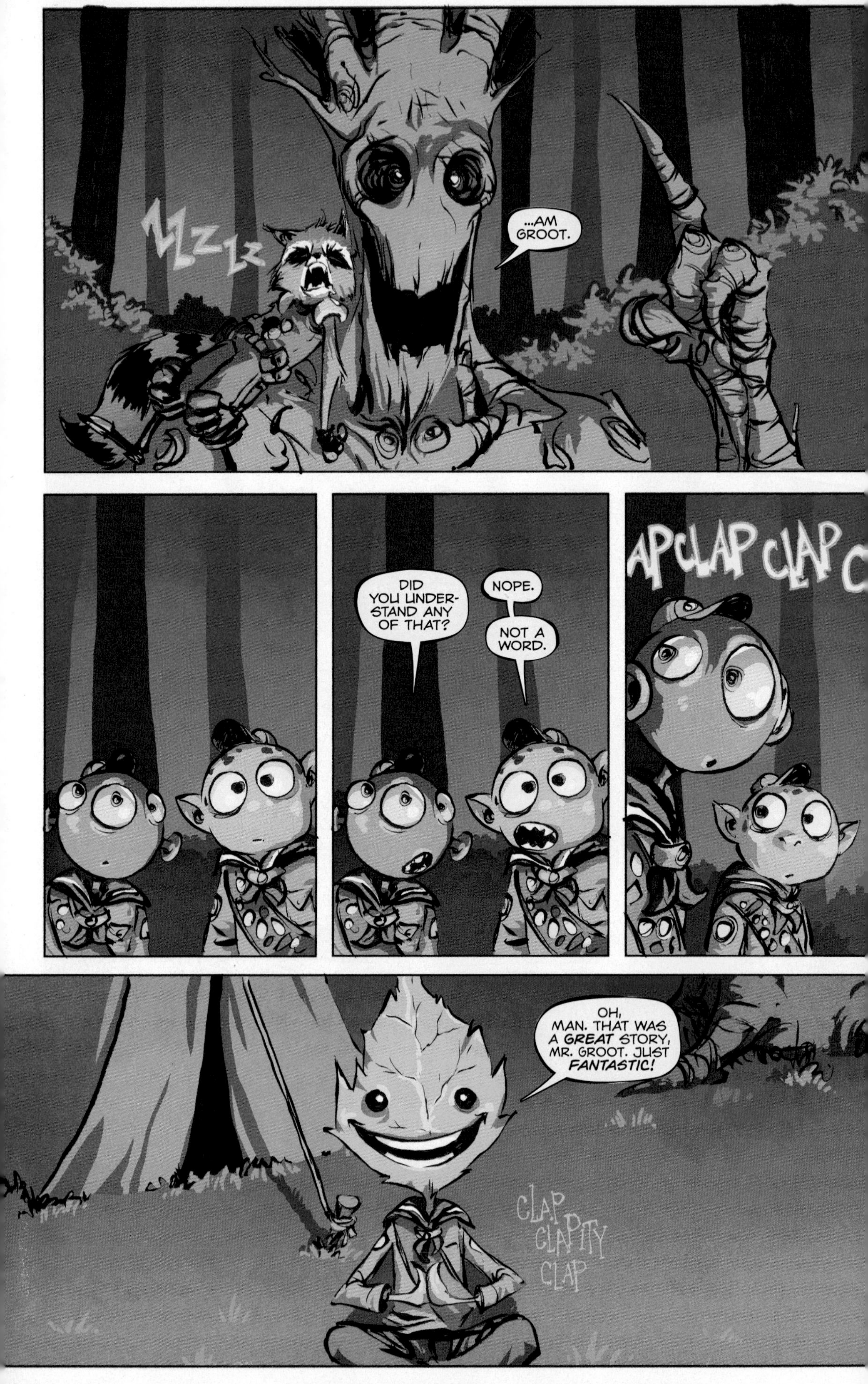
ZZZZZ
...AM GROOT.
DID YOU UNDER-STAND ANY OF THAT?
NOPE.
NOT A WORD.
APCLAP CLAP C
OH, MAN. THAT WAS A **GREAT** STORY, MR. GROOT. JUST ***FANTASTIC!***
CLAP CLAPITY CLAP

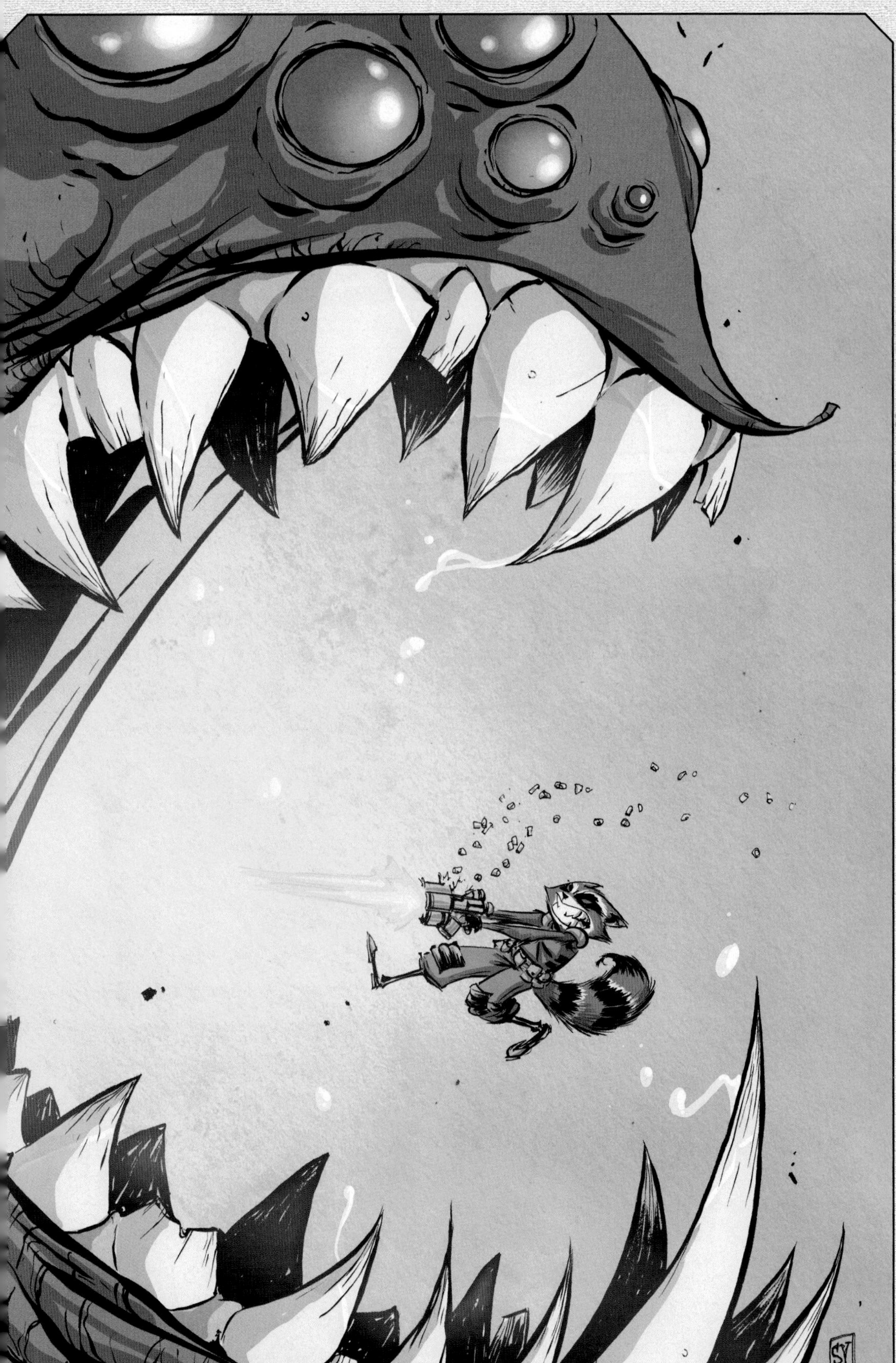
SY
14

KNOWHERE. A PORT OF CALL NEAR THE END OF THE UNIVERSE. ALSO THE SEVERED HEAD OF AN ANCIENT CELESTIAL...SO YEAH, GROSS.

THIS TRIP IS INVOLVING WAY TOO MANY PLANET-SIZED HEADS.

COSMO, I KNOW YOU HELPED US OUT ON OBLITUS*, BUT I'M PRETTY SURE LITTLE NOVA WAS GONNA PAY BACK FOR BOTH OF US.

SAM WILL MAKE FAVOR GOOD ON HIS OWN. BUT YOU NOT PUSH YOURS OFF ON CHILD. THAT IS WEAK, NO?

FINE. BUT YOU NEED TO CHANGE YOUR OUTFIT, MAN. SERIOUSLY.

WHAT DO YOU NEED?

IT'S NOT ME THAT NEEDS. IT'S A FRIEND THAT YOU HAVE THINGS IN COMMON FROM.

*Back in Nova 20, Cosmonauts!
-Deductive Dev

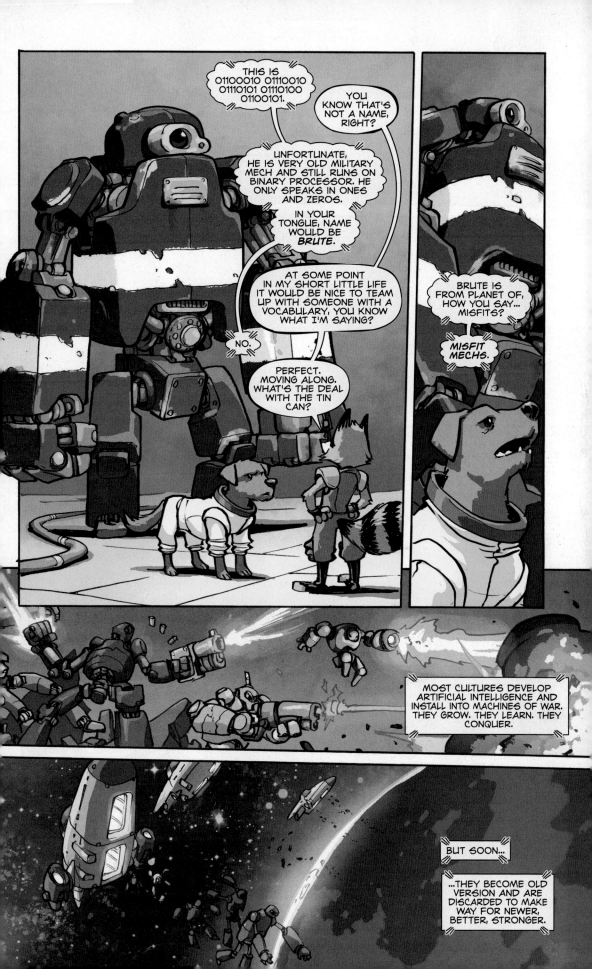

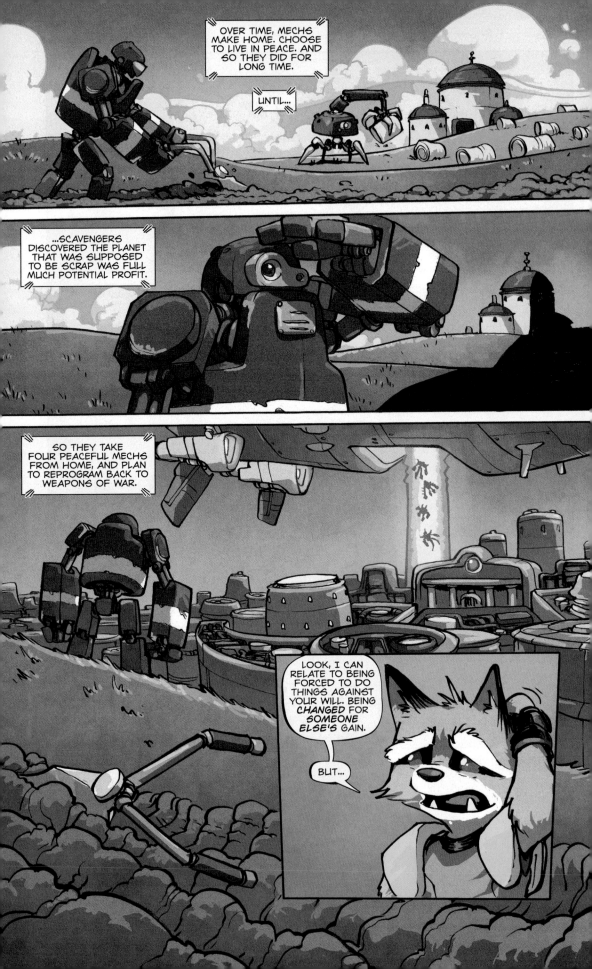

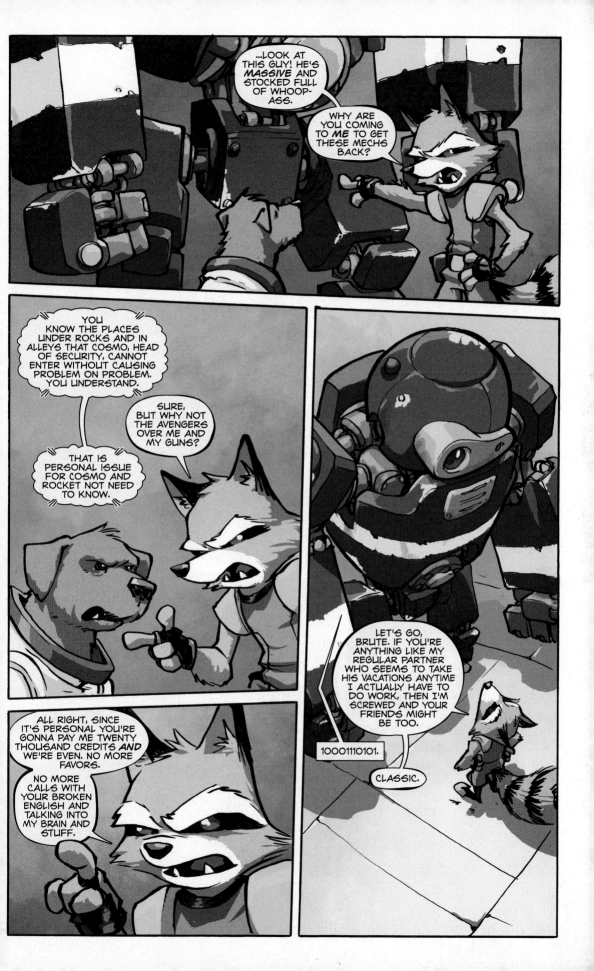

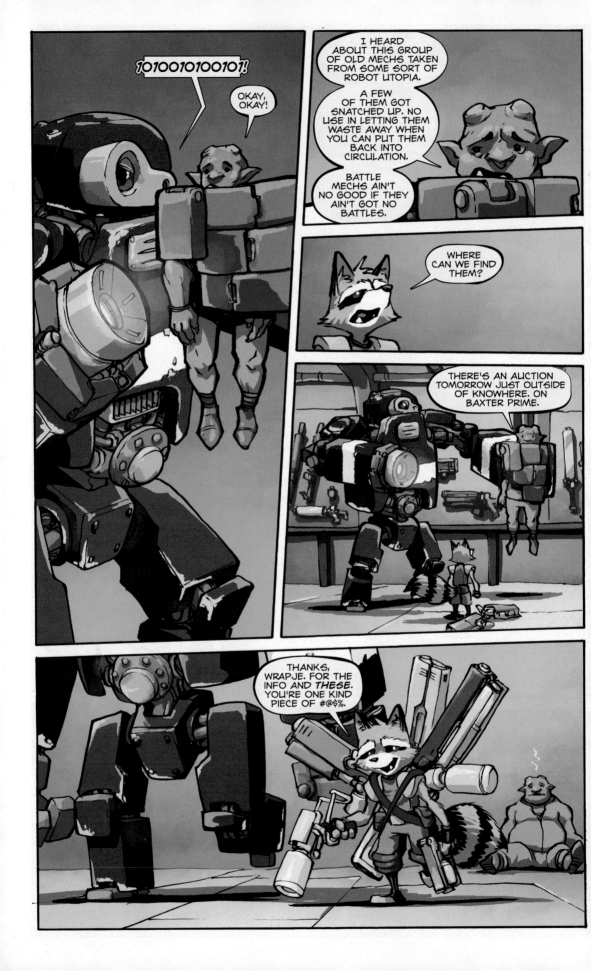

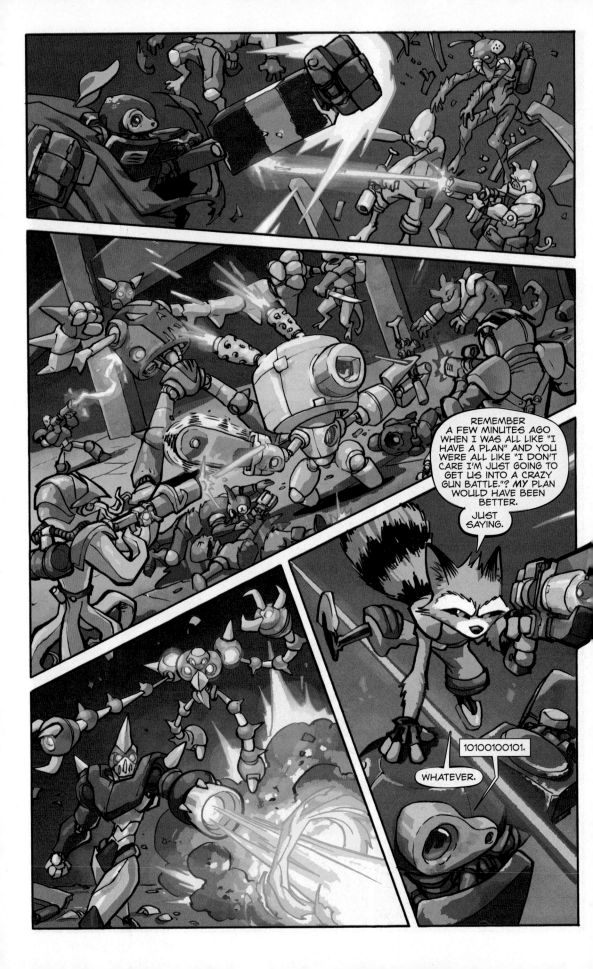

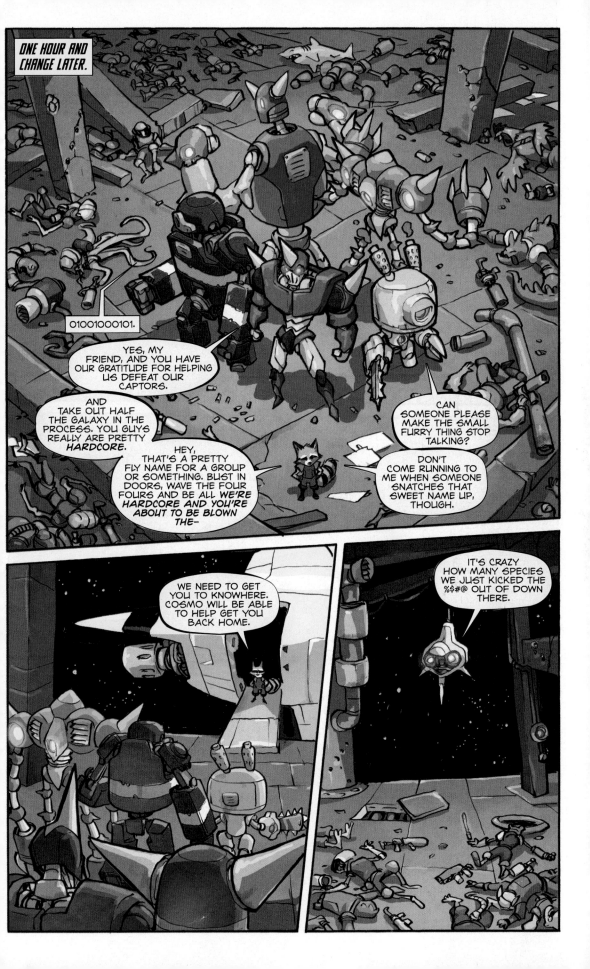

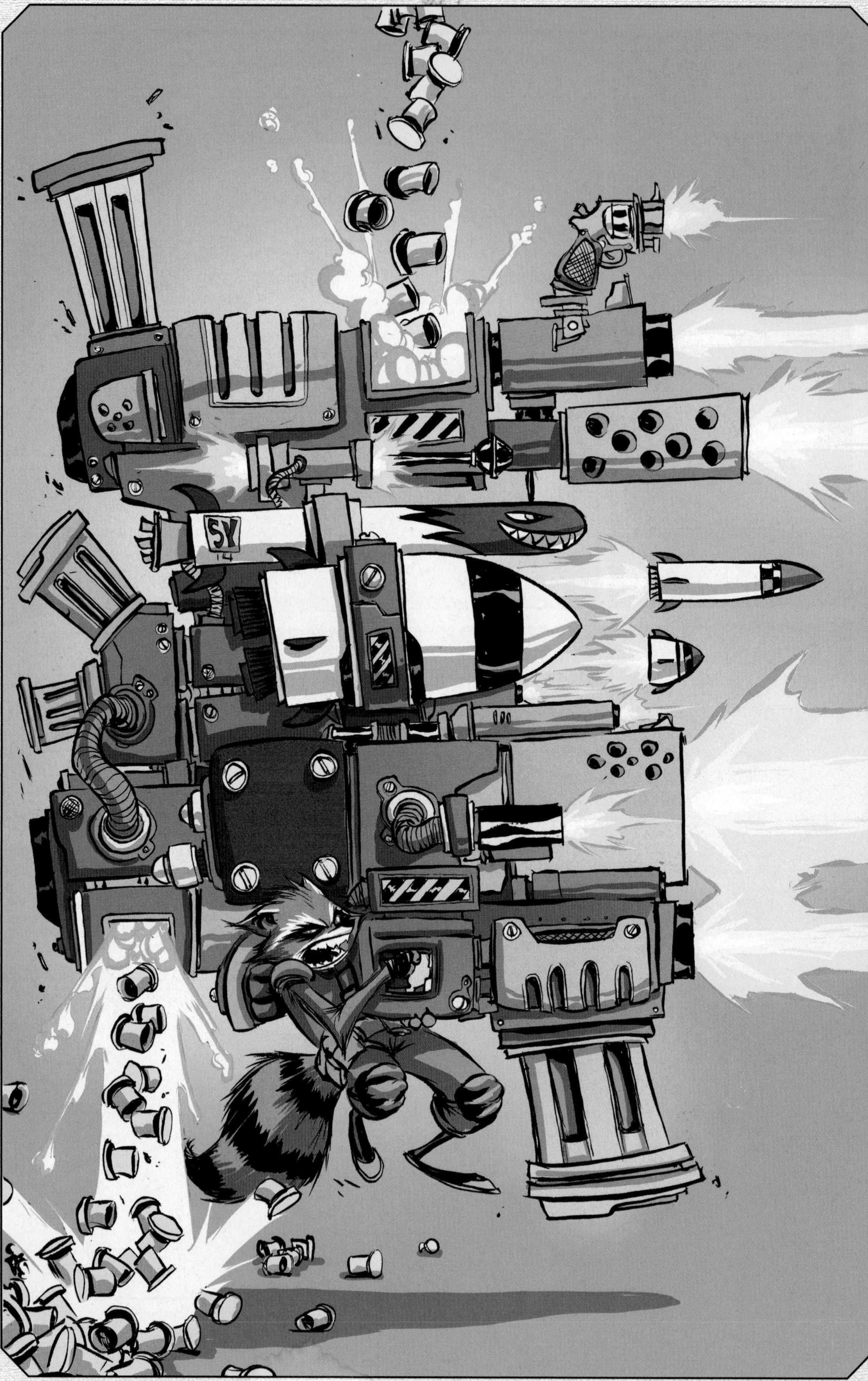
SY

ROCKET RACCOON #1 VARIANT
BY SKOTTIE YOUNG

ROCKET RACCOON #1 SDCC VARIANT
BY JEFF SMITH & TOM GAADT

ROCKET RACCOON #1 STAN LEE LEGO VARIANT
BY LEONEL CASTELLANI

ROCKET RACCOON #1 VARIANT
BY DAVID PETERSON

ROCKET RACCOON #1 MU PLUS VARIANT
BY SARAH PICHELLI & JUSTIN PONSOR

ROCKET RACCOON #1 MOVIE VARIANT

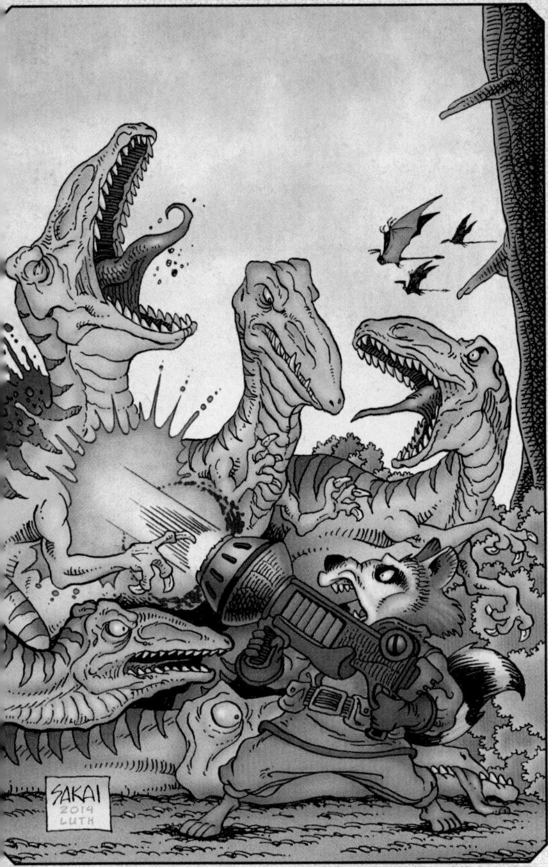
SAKAI
2014
LUTH

ROCKET RACCOON #2 VARIANT
BY STAN SAKAI & TOM LUTH

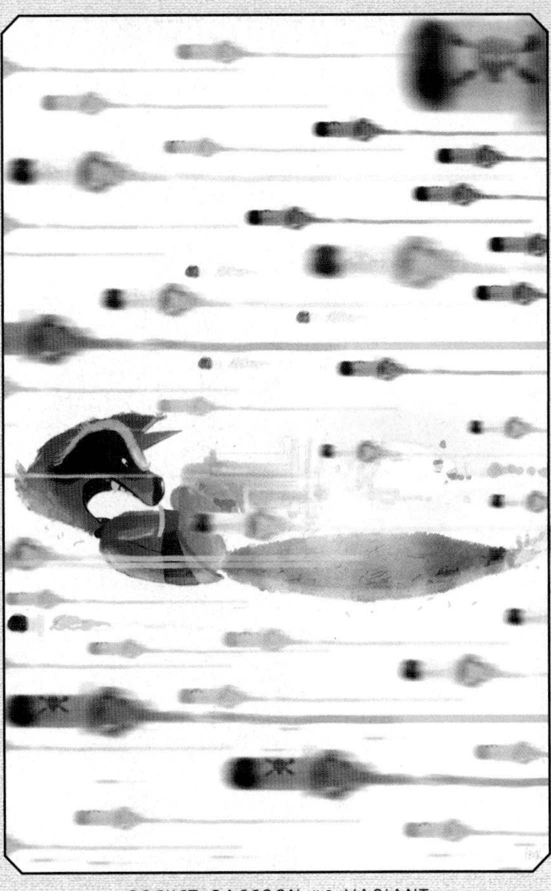

ROCKET RACCOON #3 VARIANT
BY PASCAL CAMPION

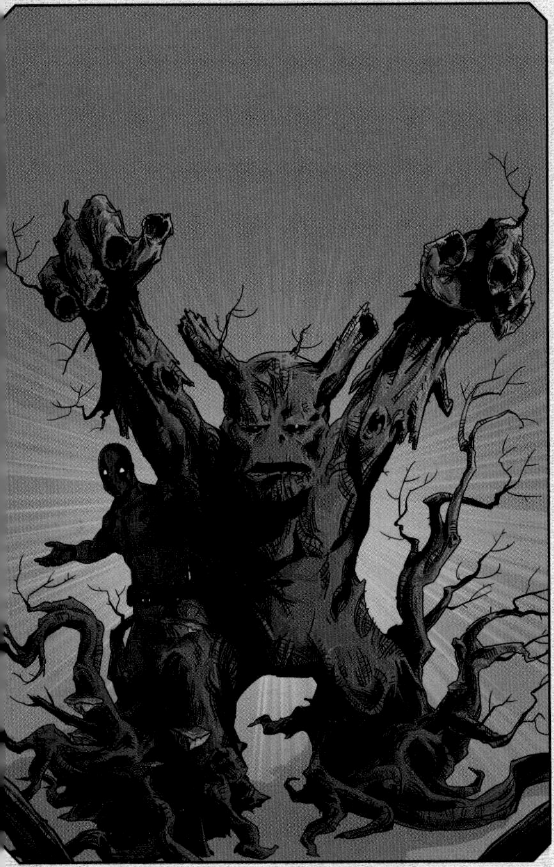

ROCKET RACCOON #4 DEADPOOL 75TH ANNIVERSARY VARIANT
BY KALMAN ANDRASOFSZKY

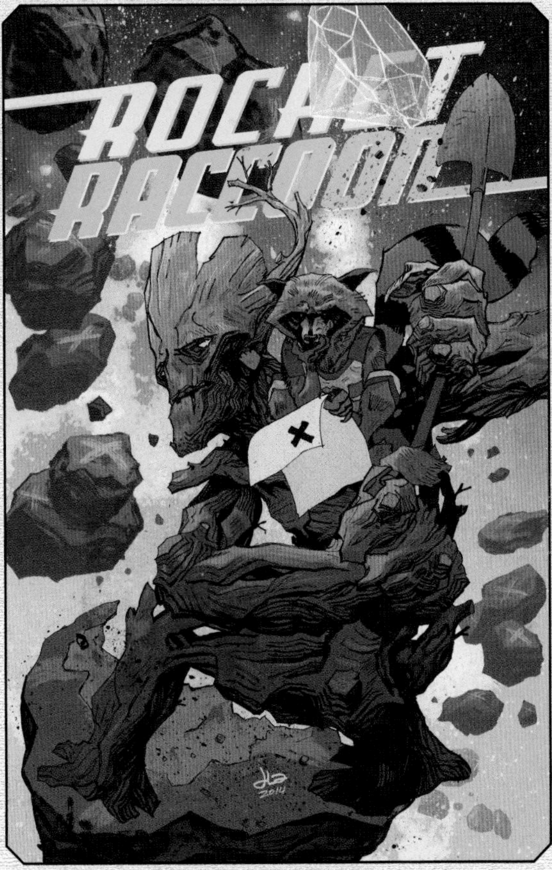

ROCKET RACCOON #5 VARIANT
BY JASON LATOUR

"IT'S GORGEOUS, WELL PLOTTED, CAPTIVATING, AND ONE OF THE BEST COMICS I'VE READ THIS YEAR." – *SuperHeroHype.com*

New York Times Best Seller!
GUARDIANS OF THE GALAXY
"This book is exciting, fresh and new." — ComicBookResources.com
COSMIC AVENGERS
BENDIS
MARVEL NOW!
McNIVEN
PICHELLI

GUARDIANS OF THE GALAXY VOL. 1: COSMIC AVENGERS

978-0-7851-6607-8 • JAN140800

MARVEL NOW!

MARVEL FREE DIGITAL COPY OFFER

TO REDEEM YOUR CODE FOR A FREE DIGITAL COPY:

1. GO TO MARVEL.COM/REDEEM. OFFER EXPIRES ON 2/11/17.
2. FOLLOW THE ON-SCREEN INSTRUCTIONS TO REDEEM YOUR DIGITAL COPY.
3. LAUNCH THE MARVEL COMICS APP TO READ YOUR COMIC NOW!
4. YOUR DIGITAL COPY WILL BE FOUND UNDER THE *MY COMICS* TAB.
5. READ & ENJOY!

YOUR FREE DIGITAL COPY WILL BE AVAILABLE ON

MARVEL COMICS APP FOR APPLE® iOS DEVICES

MARVEL COMICS APP FOR ANDROID™ DEVICES